Bannau Brycheiniog

National Park

Nick Jenkins

GRAFFEG

Bannau Brycheiniog National Park. Published in Great Britain in 2024 by Graffeg Limited. Photographed by Nick Jenkins, copyright © 2024. Designed and produced by Graffeg Limited copyright © 2024.

Graffeg Limited, 24 Stradey Park Business Centre, Mwrwg Road, Llangennech, Llanelli, Carmarthenshire, SA14 8YP, Wales, UK. Tel: 01554 824000. www.graffeg.com.

Nick Jenkins is hereby identified as the author of this work in accordance with section 77 of the Copyright, Designs and Patents Act 1988.

A CIP Catalogue record for this book is available from the British Library.

The publisher gratefully acknowledges the financial support of this book by the Books Council of Wales. www.gwales.com.

ISBN 9781802582031

1 2 3 4 5 6 7 8 9

Bannau Brycheiniog

The Name Change

Brecon Beacons National Park has officially changed its name to Bannau Brycheiniog. Pronounced ban-aye bruch-ay-nee-og, the new name translates as 'The Peaks of Brychan's Kingdom', Brychan being a legendary king who is said to have ruled the area during the 5th century. Bannau Brycheiniog has always been the Welsh name for the Park, but has now replaced the English name.

Establishment and Management

Established by the UK in 1957 as part of the post-war aim to revitalise Britain, Brecon Beacons became the third National Park in Wales. The legislative move aimed not only to conserve the natural environment but also to promote sustainable land use, recreation and education. With a total area spanning around 520 square miles of south and mid Wales, its extent includes parts of the counties of Carmarthenshire, Merthyr Tydfil, Monmouthshire, Powys and Rhondda and a diverse range of terrain, from mountains and moors to forests, lakes and pastures. Over the years, the Park has evolved into a haven for outdoor enthusiasts, offering up a varied network of trails for hikers, cyclists and nature lovers. The opportunity to visit ancient castles, Roman roads and prehistoric standing stones blends the experience of the area's natural environment with the interest of human history.

Today the Park is mostly run and managed by the Bannau

Brecon Beacons became the third National Park in Wales.

Brycheiniog National Park Authority, which owns just under 11% of the total land area and operates from its headquarters in Brecon, with over 130 staff and volunteers. The Park has an excellent visitor centre on the Mynydd Illtyd Common, which has a good cafe and excellent books and maps to read to plan your day. The Central Bannau Brycheiniog area is now owned and run by the National Trust, who work to conserve wildlife and preserve the area for the enjoyment of all and for both present and future visitors.

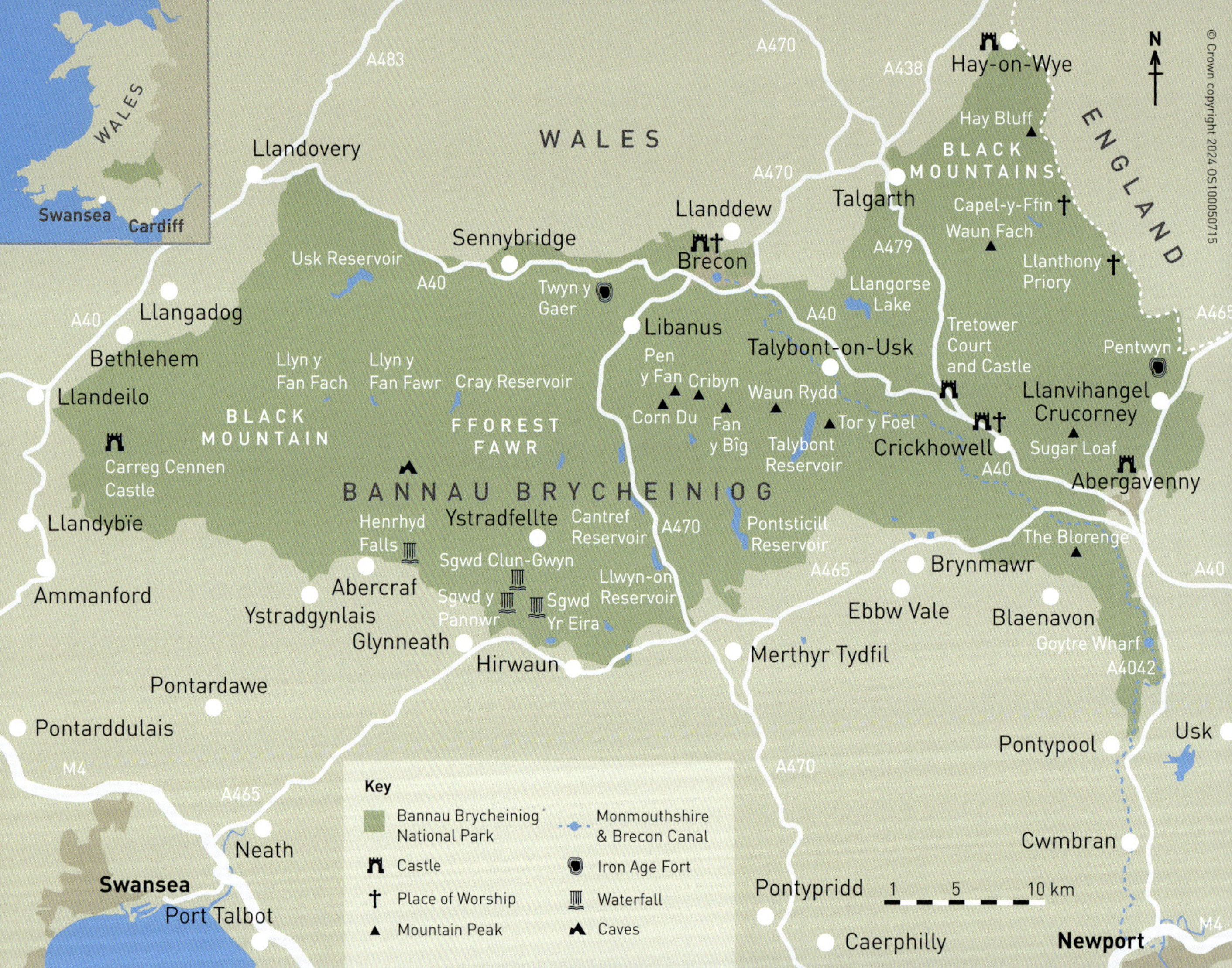

WALES
Swansea
Cardiff
© Crown copyright 2024 OS100050715
N
ENGLAND
Hay-on-Wye
Hay Bluff
BLACK MOUNTAINS
Talgarth
Capel-y-Ffin
Waun Fach
Llanthony Priory
Pentwyn
Llanvihangel Crucorney
Sugar Loaf
Abergavenny
WALES
A470
A438
A483
Llandovery
Sennybridge
Usk Reservoir
A40
Twyn y Gaer
Llanddew
Brecon
A479
Llangorse Lake
A40
Tretower Court and Castle
Llangadog
Libanus
Talybont-on-Usk
A40
Llandeilo
Bethlehem
Llyn y Fan Fach
Llyn y Fan Fawr
Cray Reservoir
Pen y Fan
Cribyn
Waun Rydd
Corn Du
Fan y Bîg
Tor y Foel
Talybont Reservoir
Crickhowell
A465
BLACK MOUNTAIN
FFOREST FAWR
BANNAU BRYCHEINIOG
Carreg Cennen Castle
Llandybïe
Henrhyd Falls
Ystradfellte
Cantref Reservoir
A470
Pontsticill Reservoir
The Blorenge
Sgwd Clun-Gwyn
Llwyn-on Reservoir
A465
Brynmawr
Abercraf
Sgwd y Pannwr
Sgwd Yr Eira
Ammanford
Ystradgynlais
Glynneath
Hirwaun
Ebbw Vale
Blaenavon
Goytre Wharf
A4042
Merthyr Tydfil
Pontardawe
Pontarddulais
A470
Usk
Pontypool
M4
A465
Cwmbran
Neath
Swansea
Port Talbot
Pontypridd
1 5 10 km
Caerphilly
Newport
A40
Key
Bannau Brycheiniog National Park
Castle
Place of Worship
Mountain Peak
Monmouthshire & Brecon Canal
Iron Age Fort
Waterfall
Caves

In 2012 the Park became only the world's fifth International Dark Sky Reserve. The lack of light pollution here results in spectacular starry skies, with regular stargazing nights taking place during the year, as well as an annual Dark Sky Festival, which celebrates this prestigious status. The Park has also been recognised as a Geopark, a designation which highlights the area's commitment to conservation, education and sustainable tourism. Home to a fascinating geological legacy of ancient rocks and unique landforms, visitors can delve into this aspect of the area's past through guided tours and interpretive displays.

Areas of the Park and Key Features

The Park is divided into four sections: East Bannau Brycheiniog, or the Black Mountains, Central Bannau Brycheiniog, Fforest Fawr, and West Bannau Brycheiniog, or Black Mountain.

The Black Mountains, to the east of the Brecon Beacons, offer a rugged landscape characterised by rolling hills, distinctive blackened escarpments and breathtaking panoramic views of the surrounding countryside, including the Wye Valley. All OS Maps covering the Bannau Brycheiniog have footpaths clearly marked so that you can explore your chosen area with confidence. Be very aware that inclement weather can close in up here at any time, so do check the

In 2012 the Park became the world's fifth International Dark Sky Reserve.

weather forecast before you set off and ensure to take appropriate clothing in case of wind and rain, a compass and map (or access via your devices) and make sure that you or your party are aware of the route and don't deviate. Staff at the visitor centre can also provide further advice.

Central Bannau Brycheiniog has become a very popular location for all sorts of good reasons, with its steep hills and mountains attractive to keen

For some excellent views of the park across to Pen y Fan and Corn Du, Mynydd Illtyd Common is an ideal destination.

walkers and anyone who enjoys spending time outdoors, allowing visitors to appreciate both the walking route and the superb scenery that surrounds them. For some excellent views of the park across to Pen y Fan and Corn Du, Mynydd Illtyd Common is an ideal destination.

To the east are the Black Mountains, which you may find to be less crowded than Central Bannau Brycheiniog, but which nonetheless afford beautiful scenery. The Vale of Ewyas, with its famous 'out of kilter' church in the village of Cwmyoy, is always worth a visit, as well as the beautifully peaceful remains of Llanthony Priory. Further up the valley there is the monastery at Capel y Ffin (reached by a signposted left turn) and the small, whitewashed chapel referred to by the Reverend Francis Kilvert as a stout grey owl – based, I suspect, on the chapel windows.

Further up the valley the road tops out to majestic views of the Black Mountains to the left and a view of the steep path to the summit of Hay Bluff, almost on the Wales-England border. To the west are Fforest Fawr and the Black Mountain, and here the hills tend to be more remote, but are nonetheless worthy of an exploratory walk to take in the change of scenery.

Fforest Fawr is smaller and it is easy to travel its length via a road up the valley of the River Llia. To the right is Fan Llia and to the left again on the right is the Maen Llia Standing Stone. To the left is the slope of Neath Mountain or Fan Nedd. The Black Mountain is in Carmarthenshire, but is still an integral part of the Bannau Brycheiniog as a whole. Here there are two lakes, Llyn y Fan Fawr and Llyn y Fan Fach, both fairly easy to walk to and often very quiet. Here are the Bannau Brycheiniog and Picws Du, which are often used as a walk to link up the two lakes, while beyond this the park becomes lower and more agricultural and leads to the well-known Carreg Cennen castle.

Because the National Park has more day hikes than you can shake a walking stick at, the Beacons Way remains a trail for connoisseurs. This difficult long distance trail covers over 100 miles of the arguably the best but relatively little known walk in Wales between Llangadog and Abergavenny. You can take the high-ground by day then dip to towns each night, via glacial lakes, waterfalls, castles, major peaks and stunning views.

Nestled in the southern reaches of the park, Waterfall Country is renowned for its stunning waterfalls. The Four Falls Trail takes visitors on a magical journey past the waterfalls of Sgwd Clun-Gwyn, Sgwd Isaf Clun-Gwyn, Sgwd y Pannwr, and Sgwd-yr-Eira. Sgwd-yr-Eira, in particular, allows intrepid explorers to walk behind the curtain of water.

Each area of the Park is well worthy of exploration and the views from the higher summits are just stunning. Every section of the Park has its own high peaks, so explore them carefully and they will reward you with experiences to treasure. All in all, the Bannau Brycheiniog National Park is an amazing playground, so go and discover what there is on offer, and above all, have fun!

Nick Jenkins

Every section of the Park has its own high peaks, so explore them carefully and they will reward you with experiences to treasure.

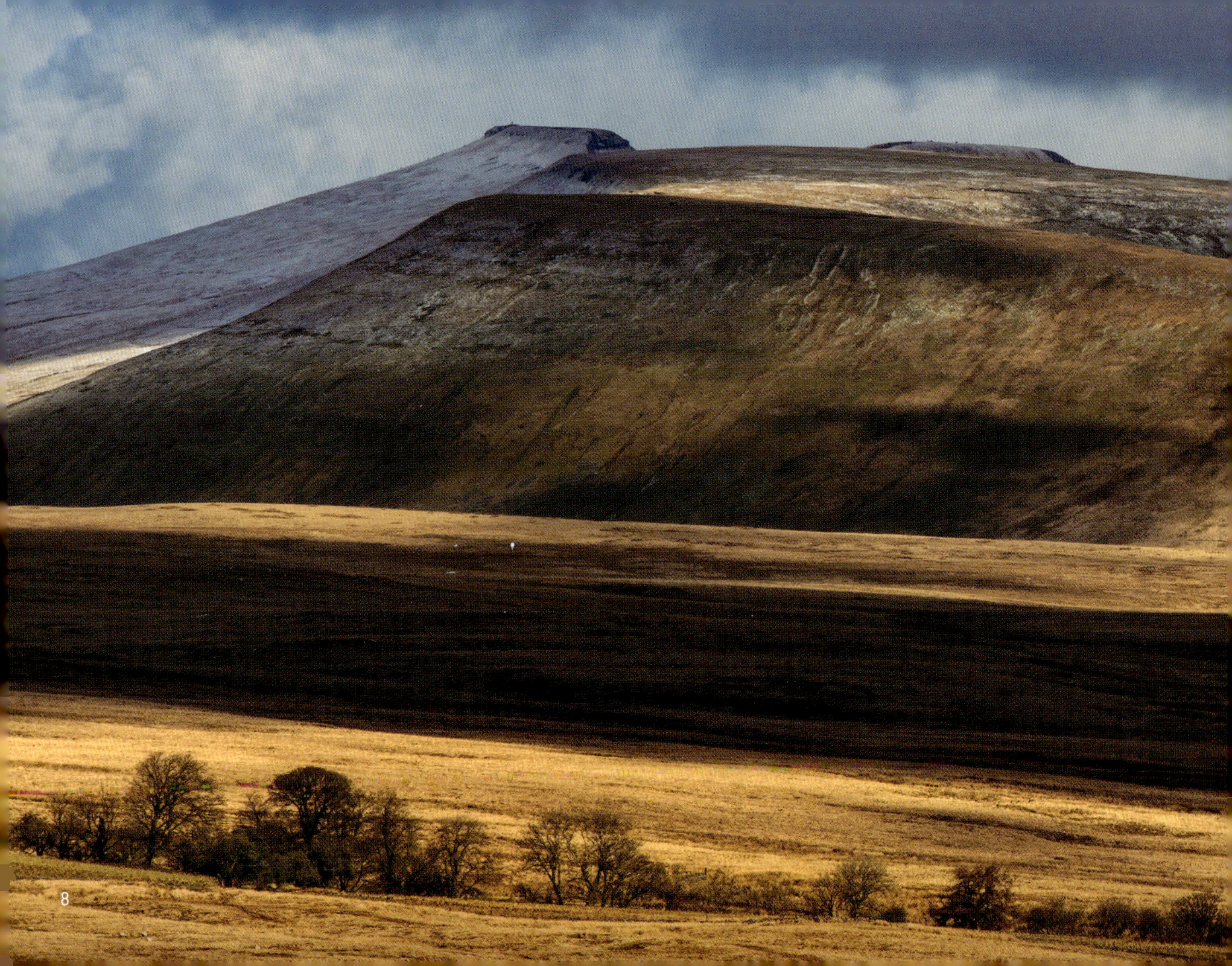

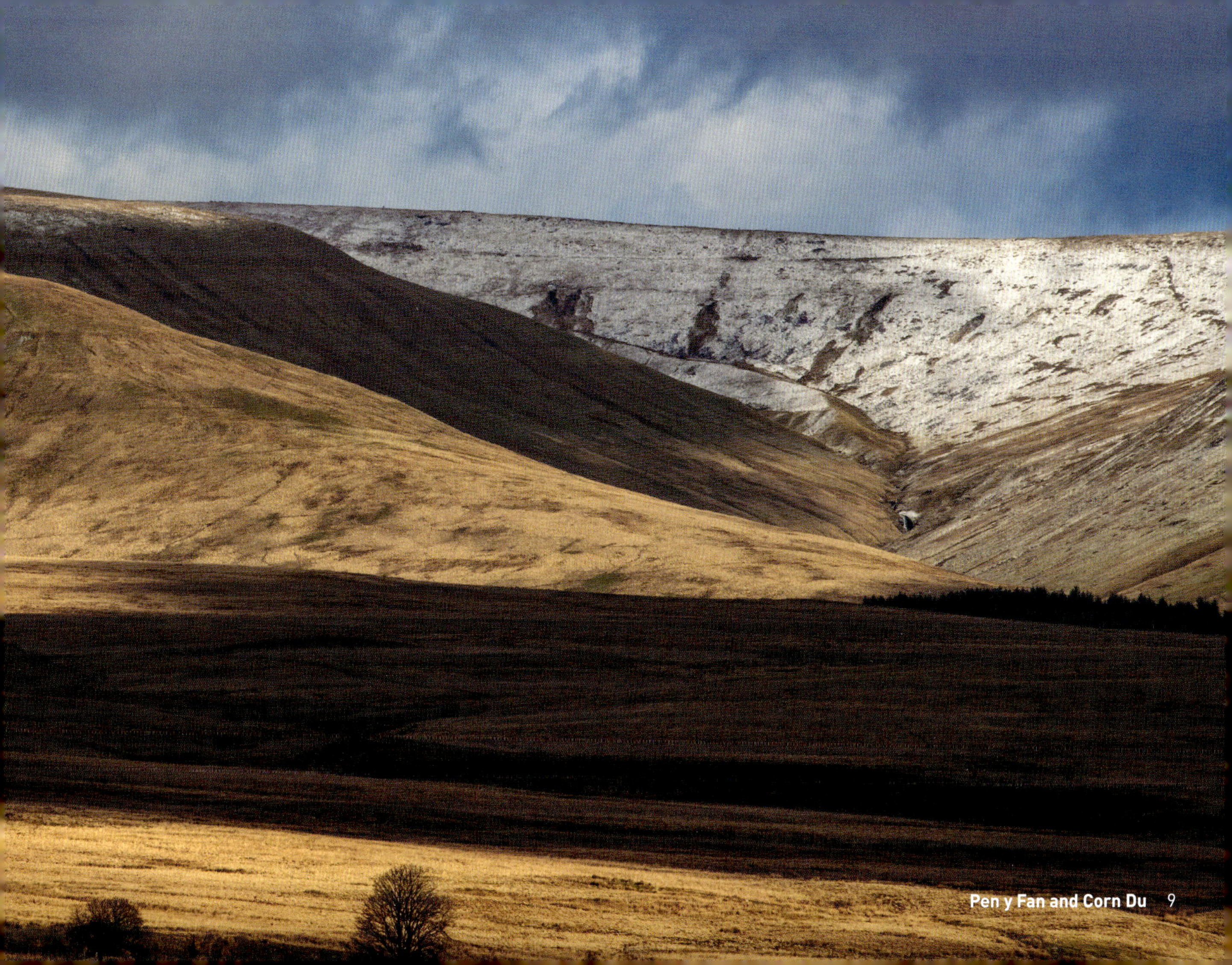
Pen y Fan and Corn Du 9

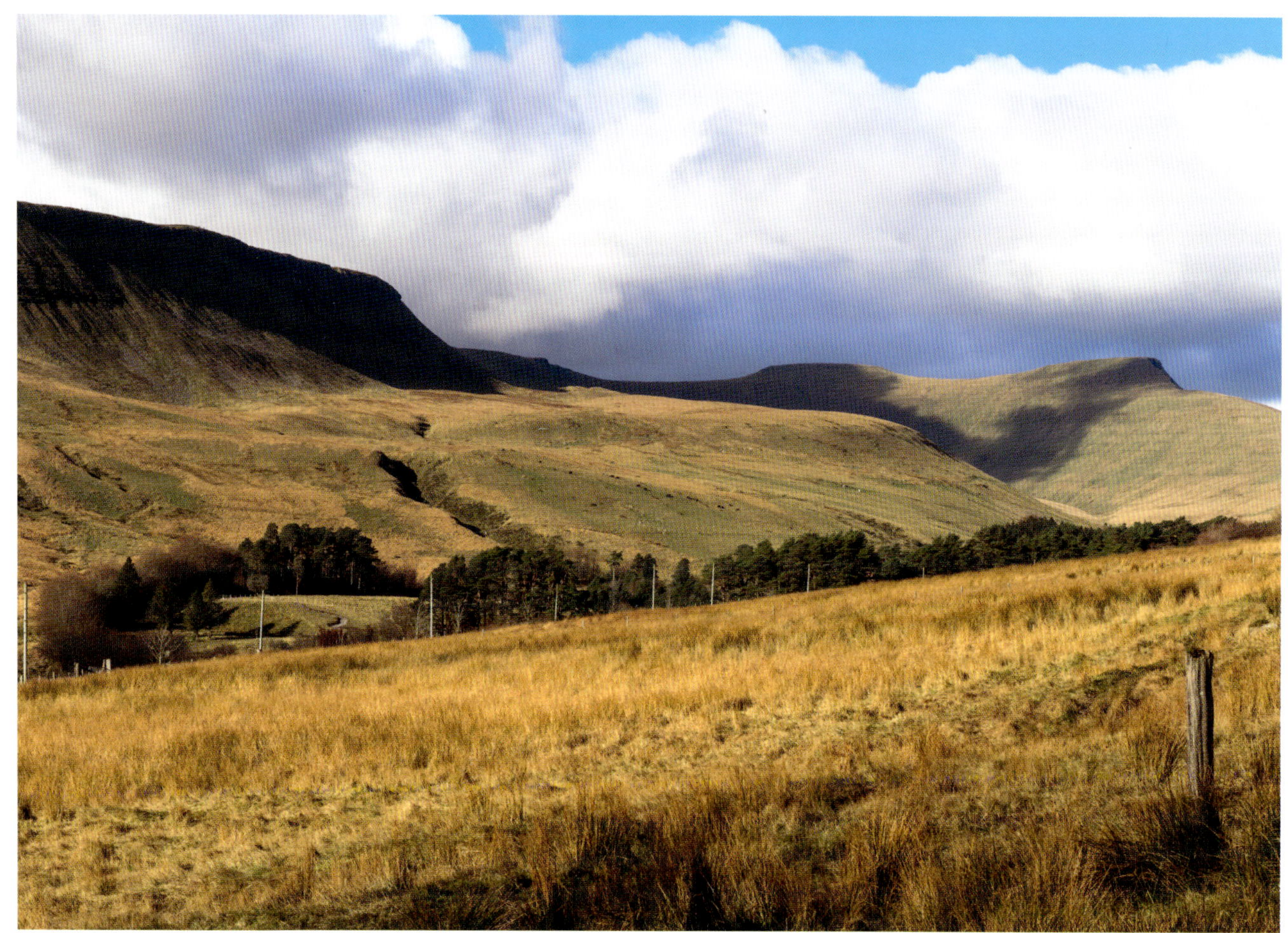

 Graig Fan Ddu, Corn Du and Pen y Fan

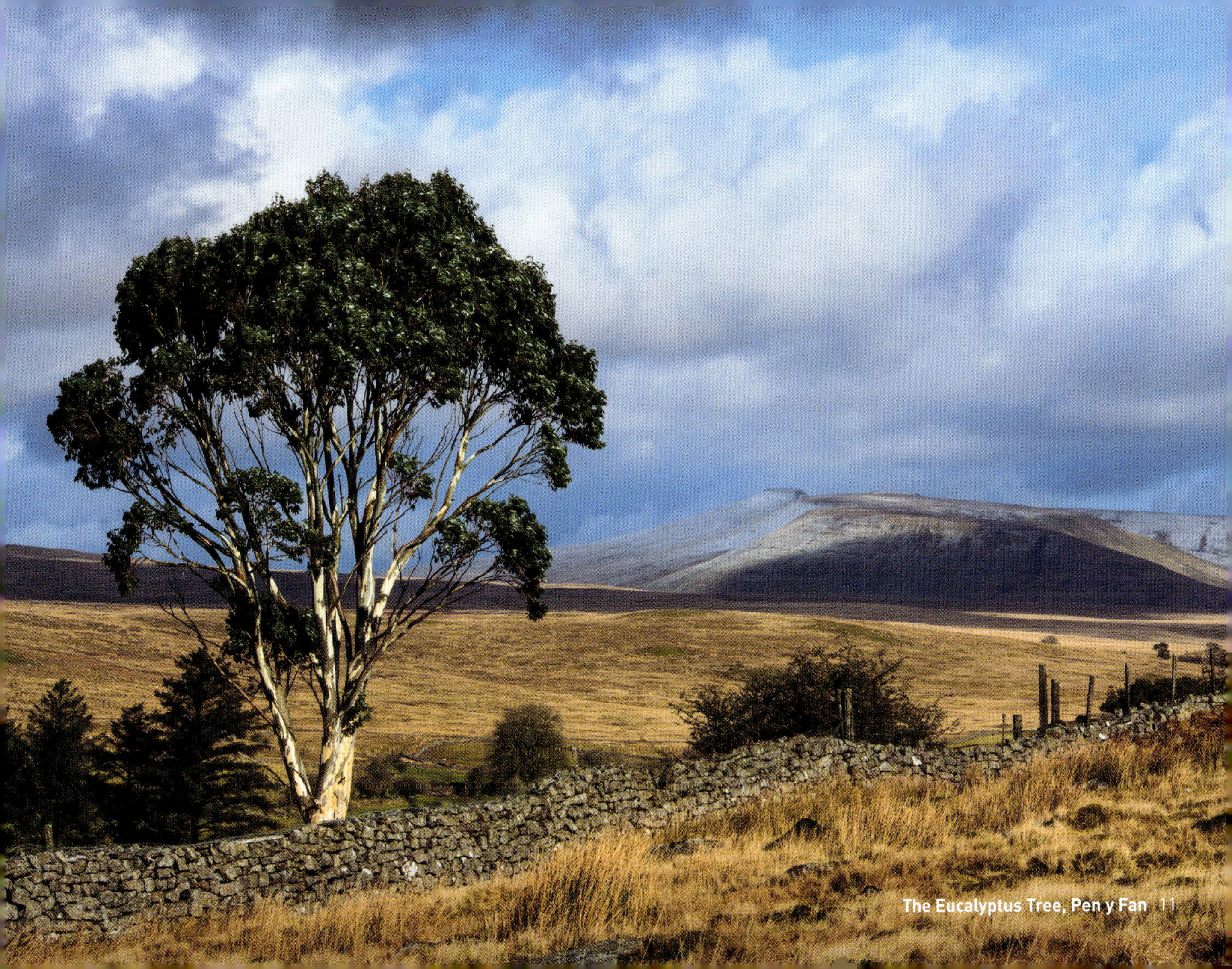

The Eucalyptus Tree, Pen y Fan 11

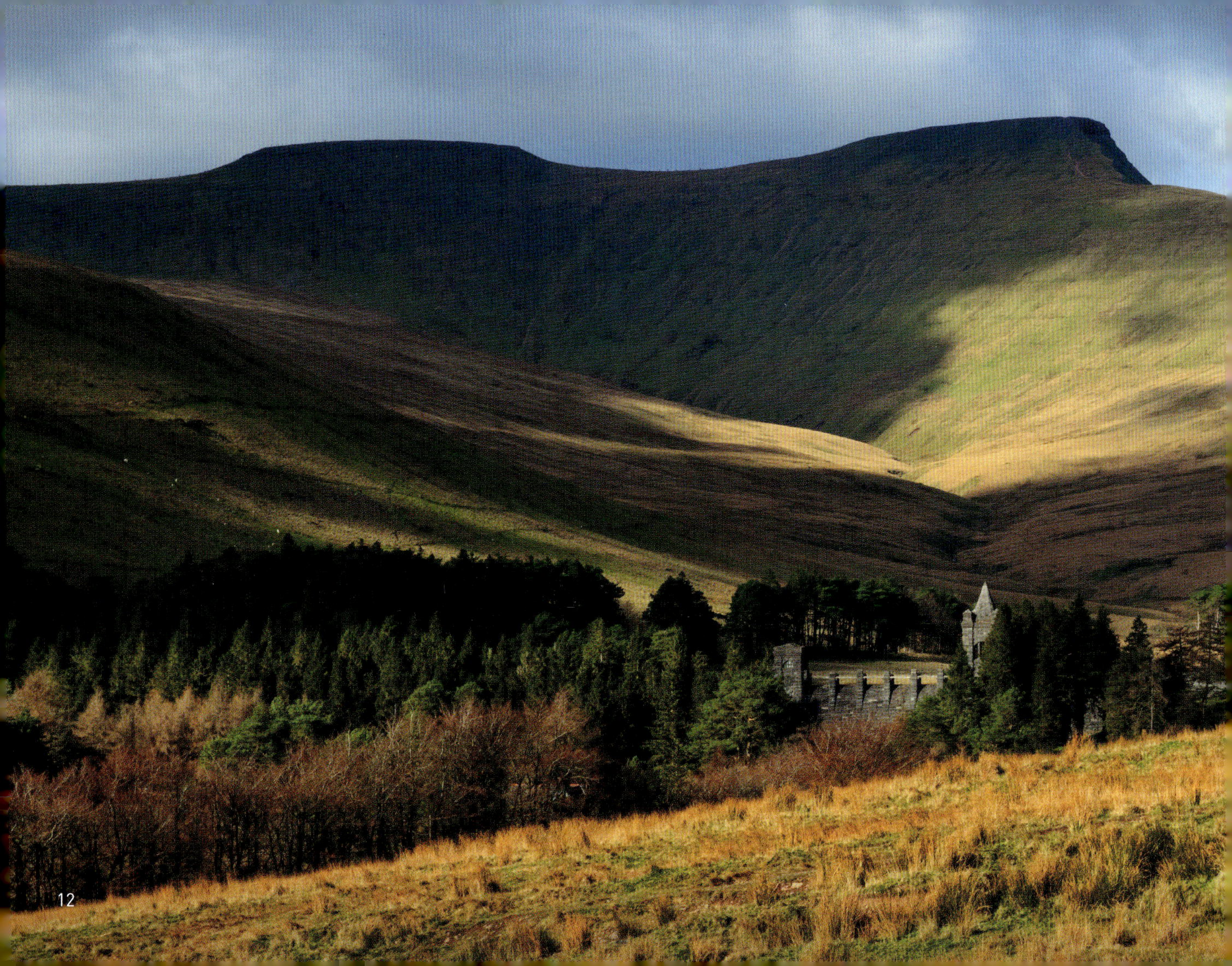

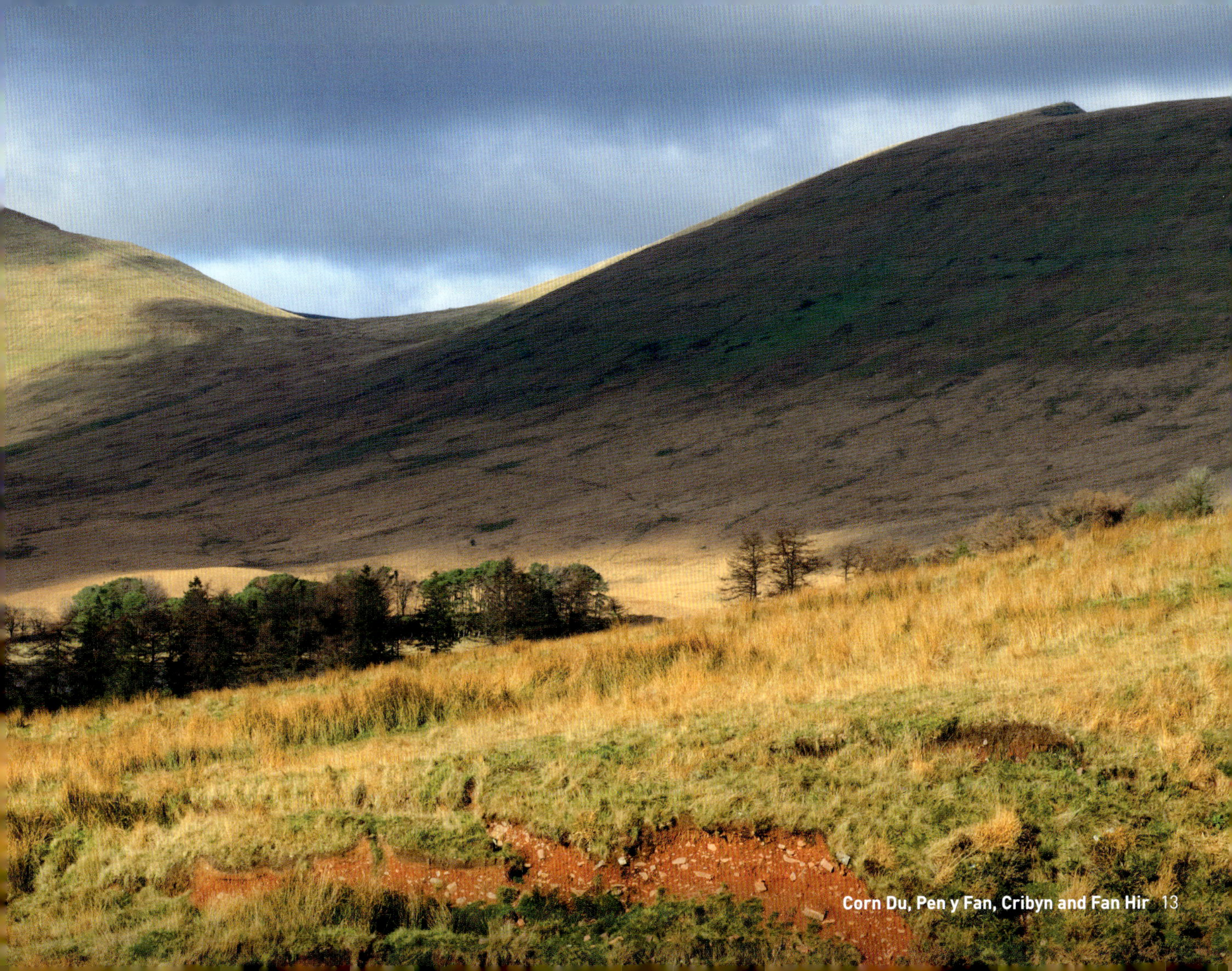
Corn Du, Pen y Fan, Cribyn and Fan Hir 13

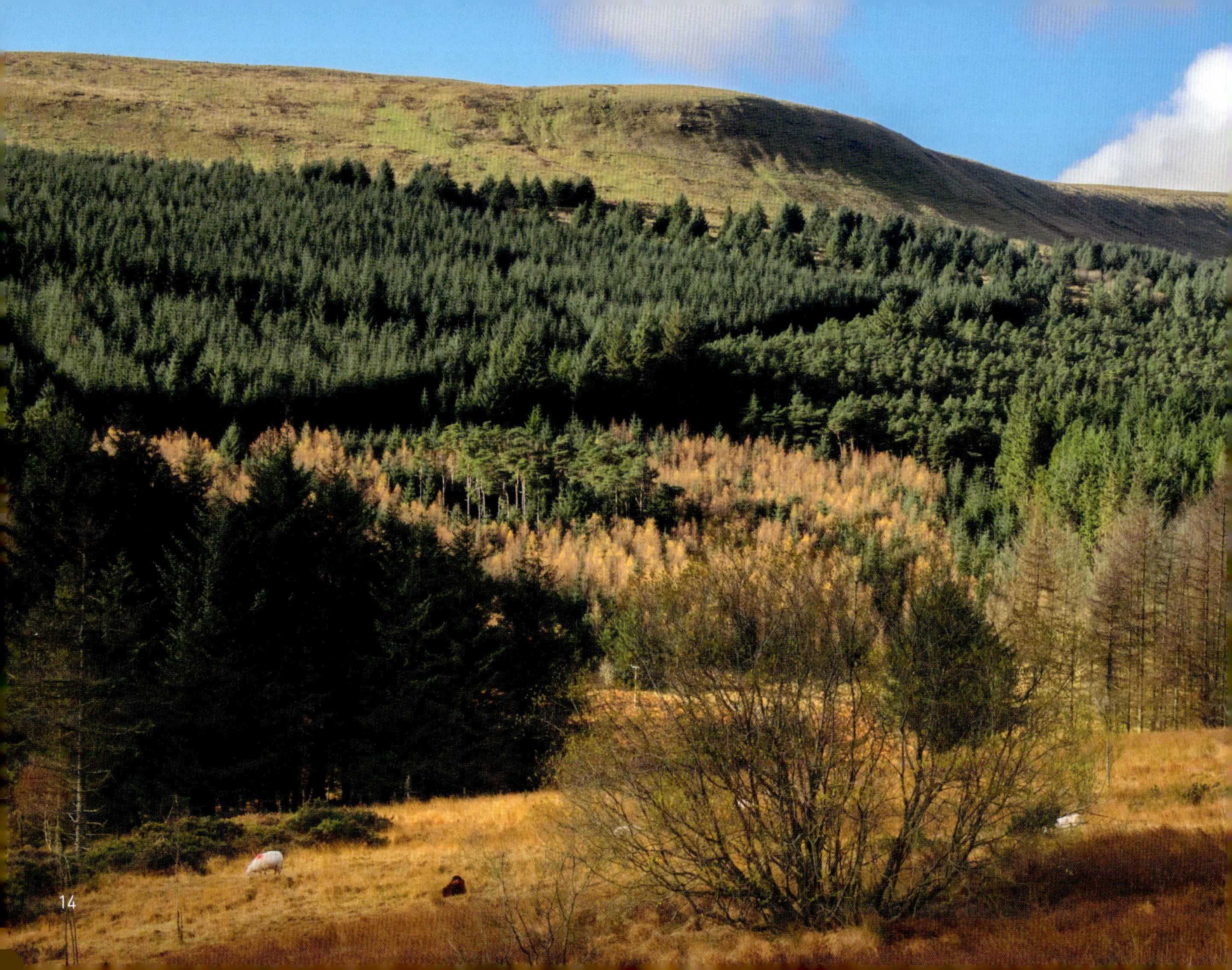

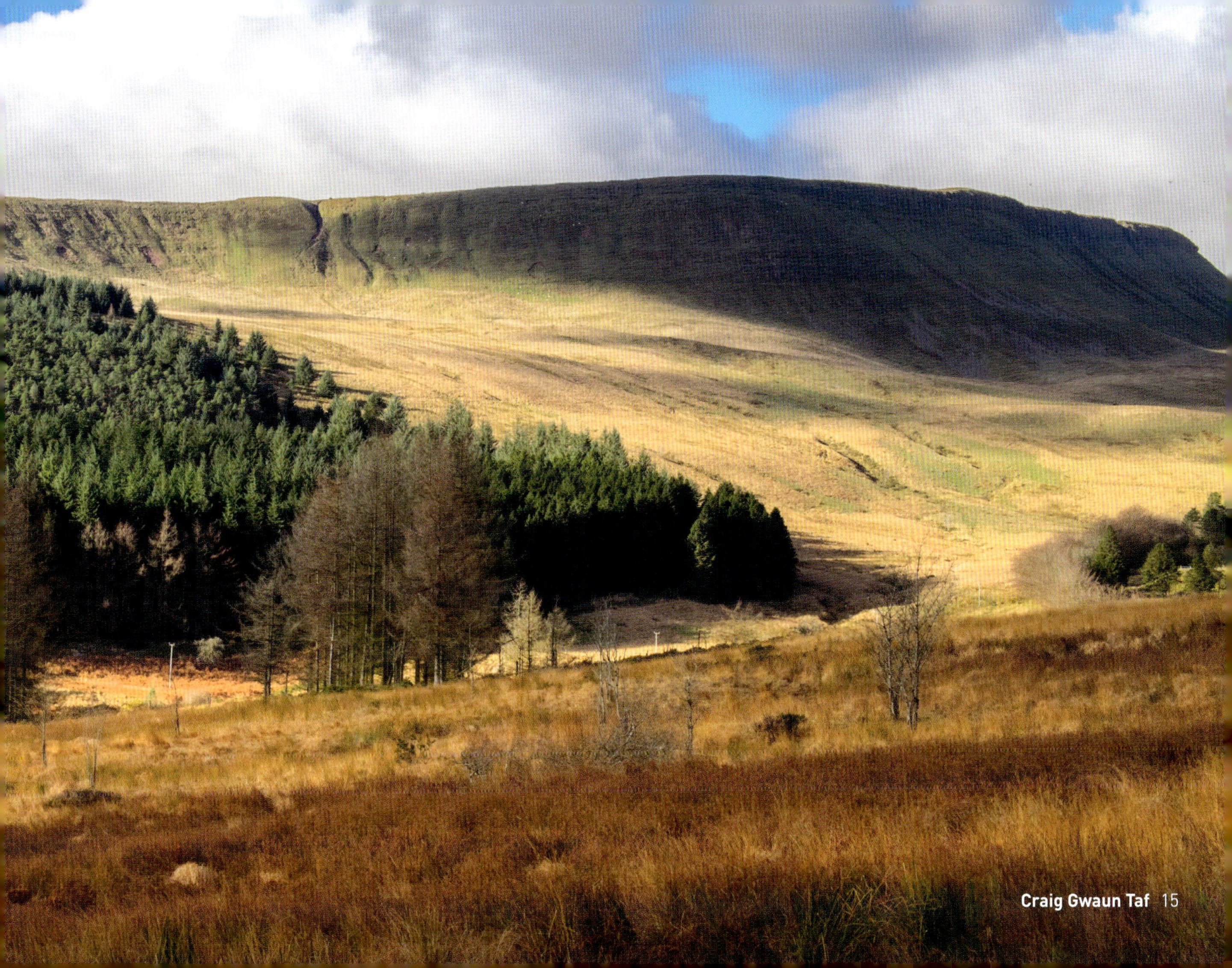

Craig Gwaun Taf 15

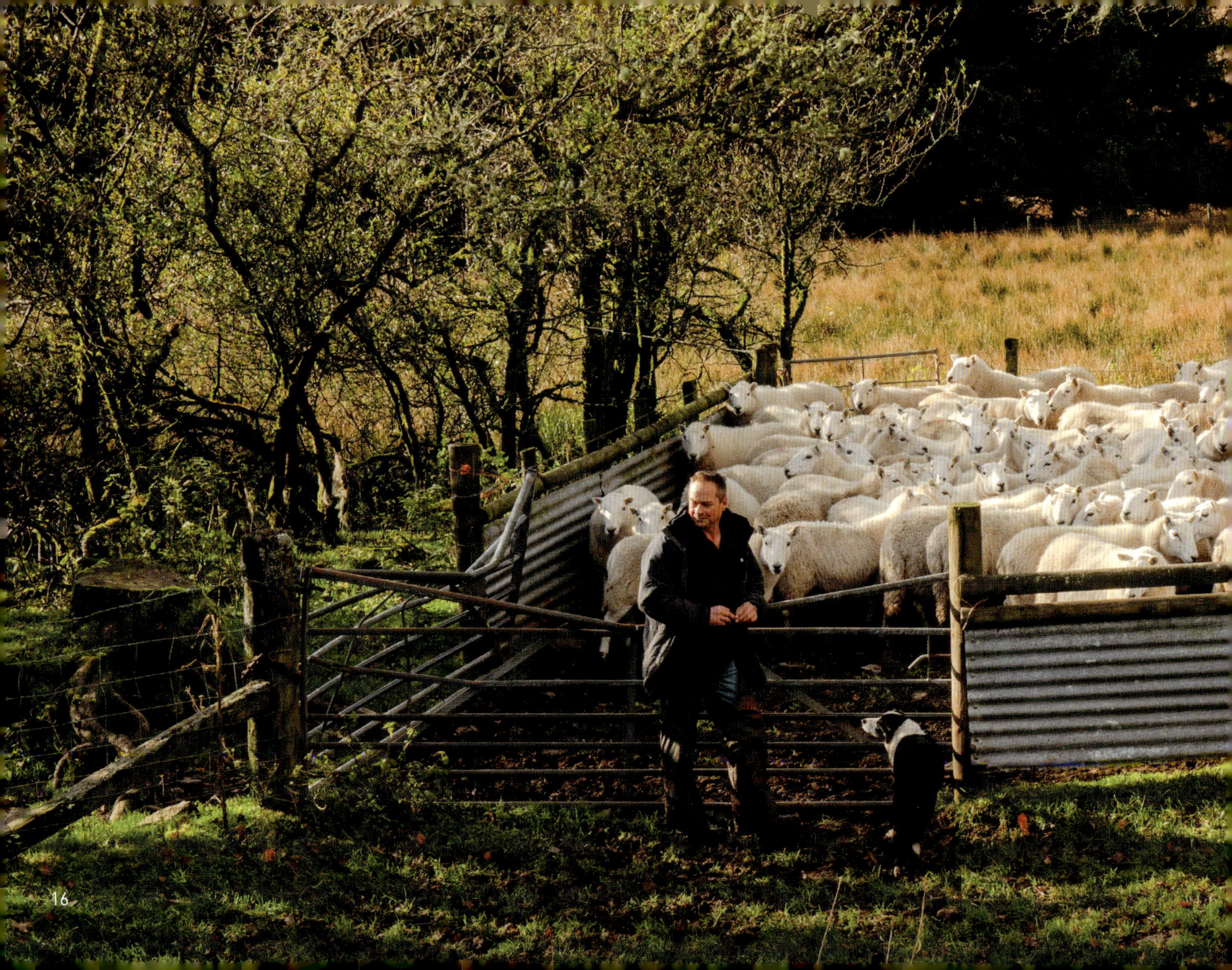

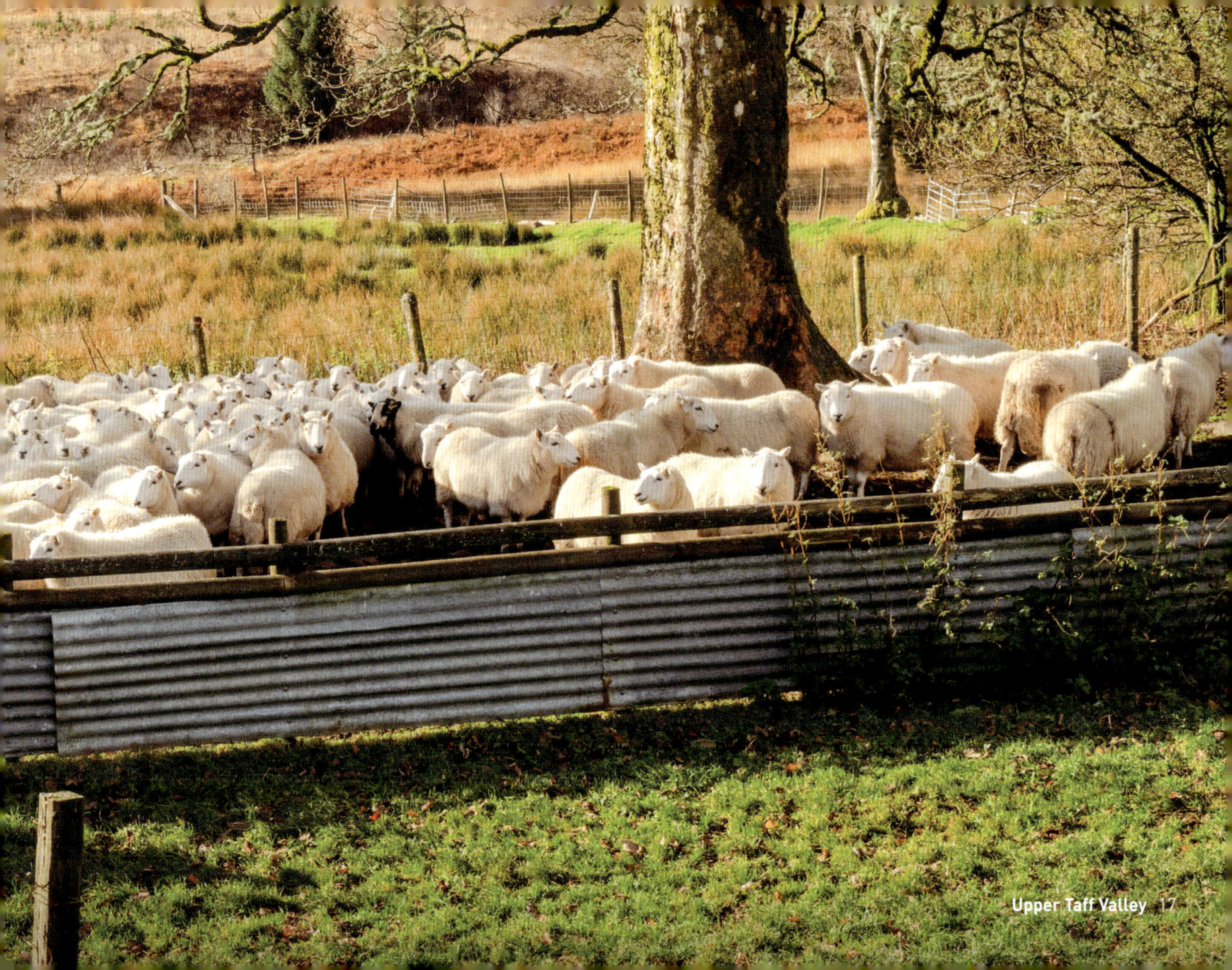

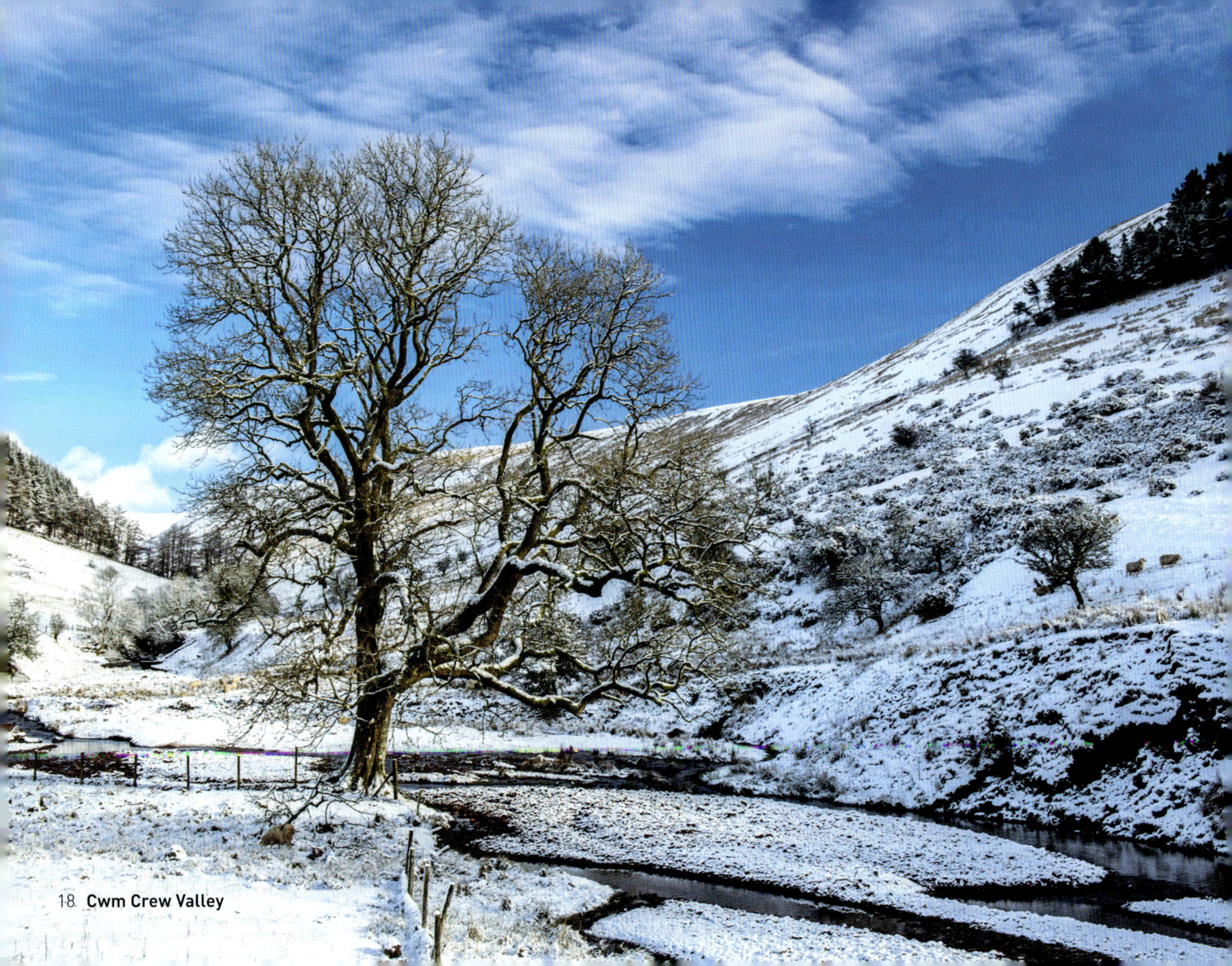

18 **Cwm Crew Valley**

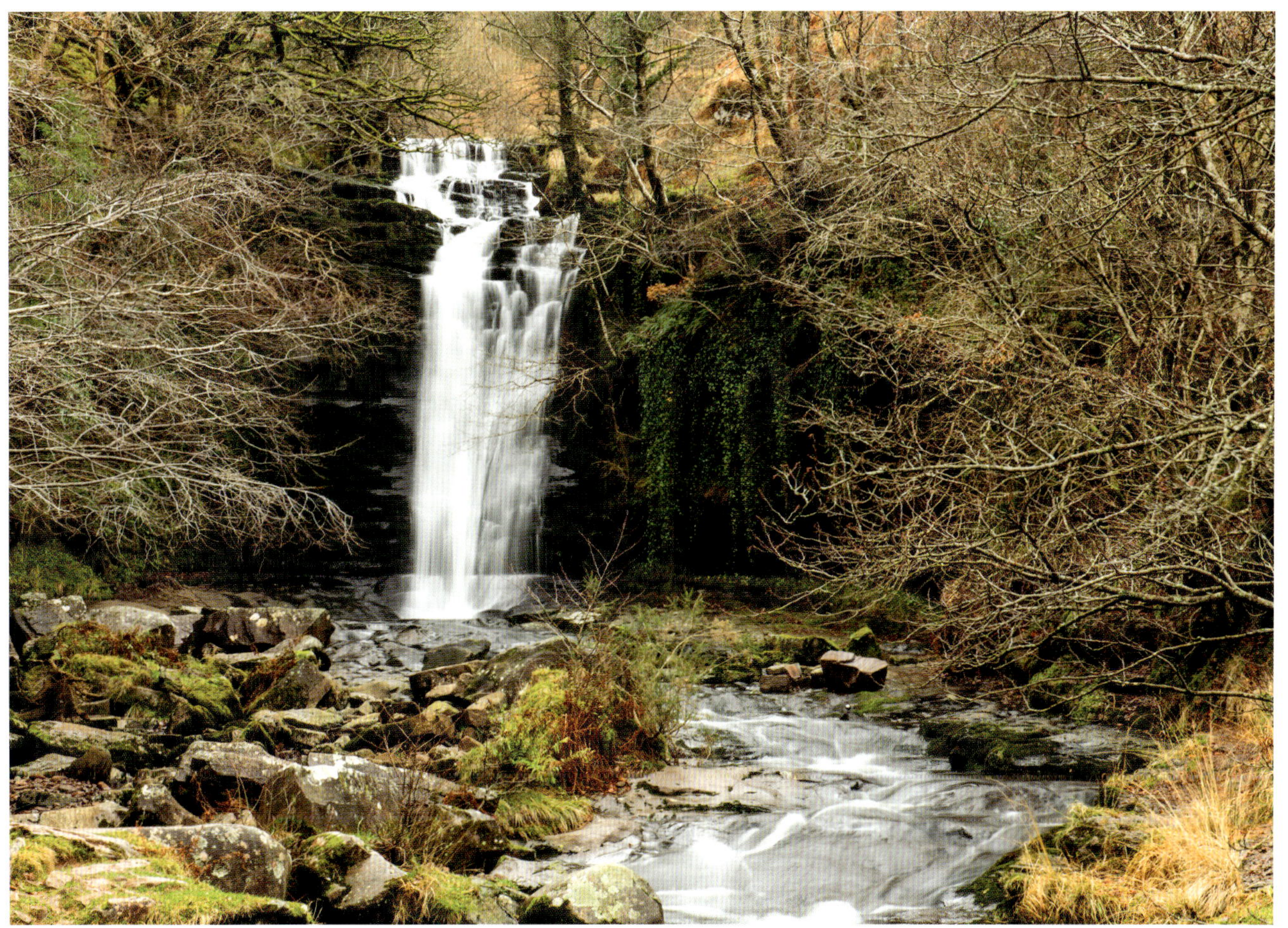

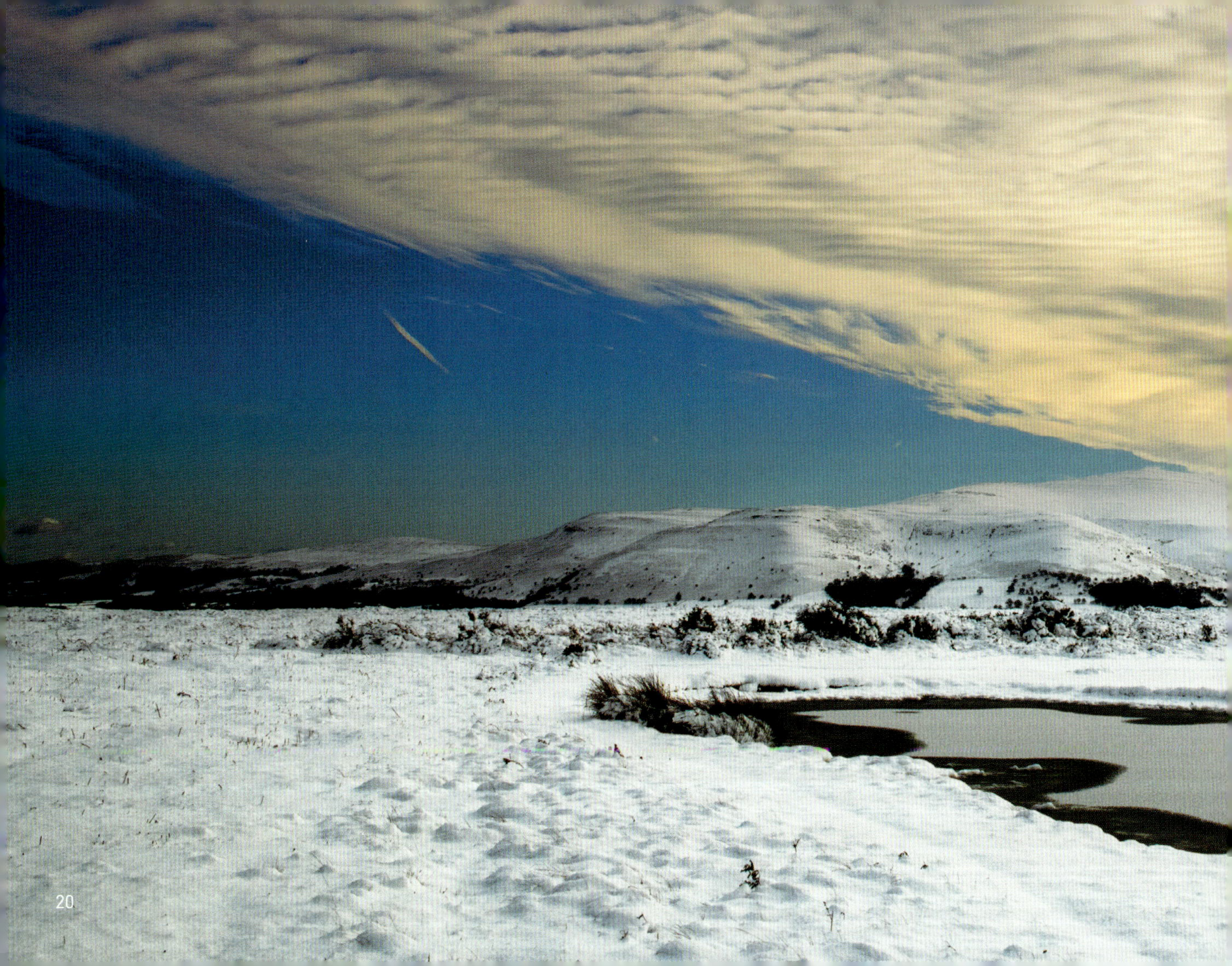

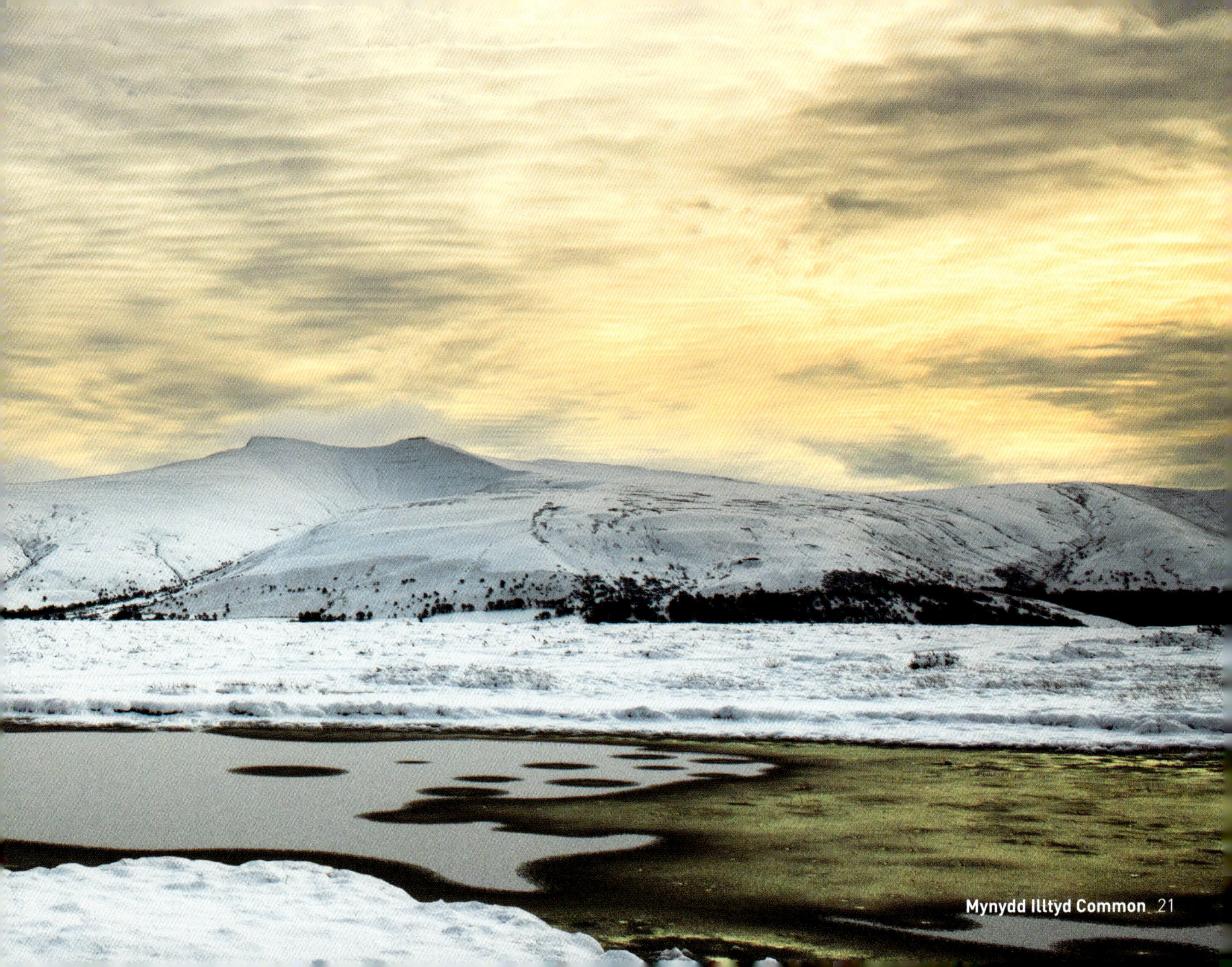

Mynydd Illtyd Common 21

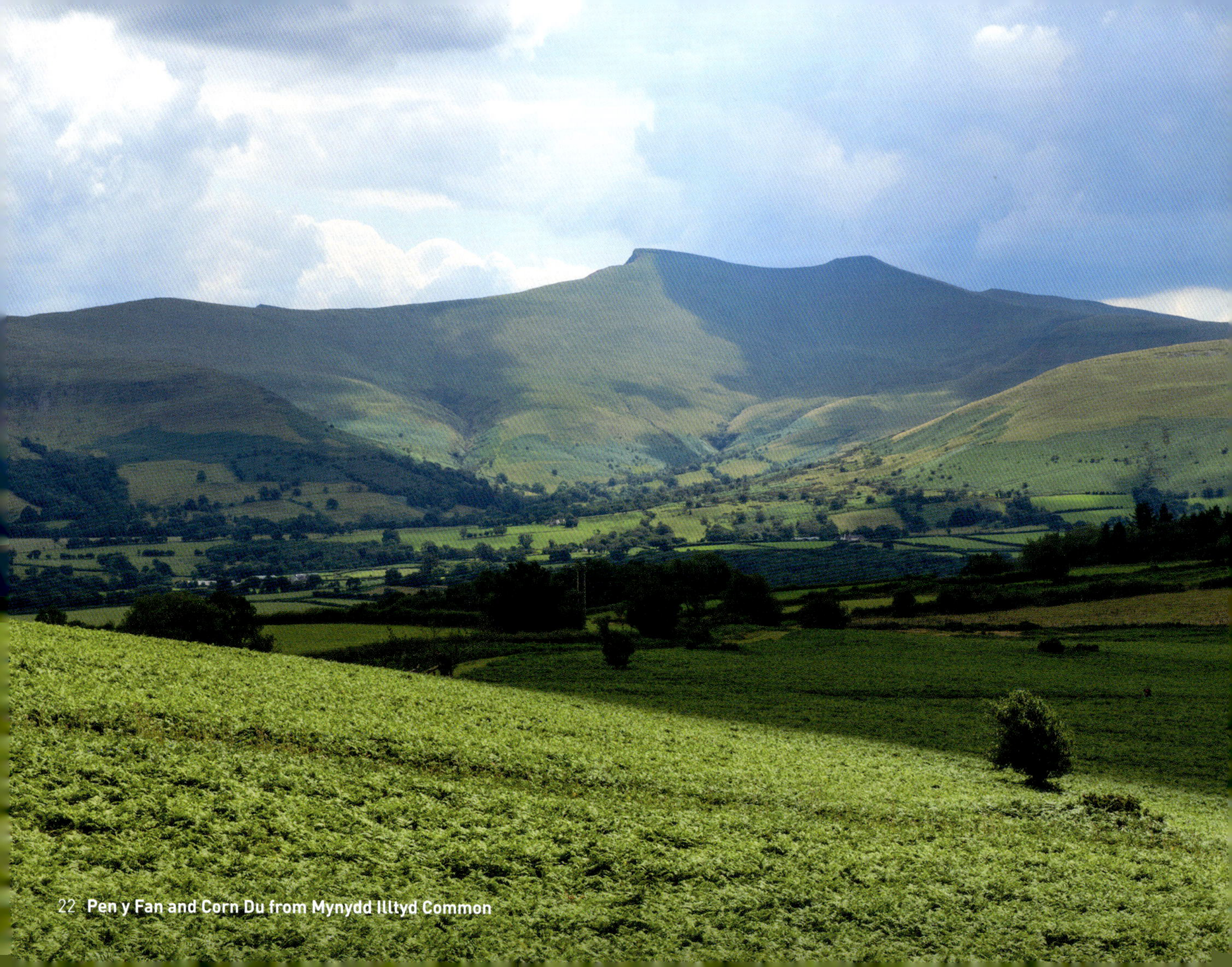
22 Pen y Fan and Corn Du from Mynydd Illtyd Common

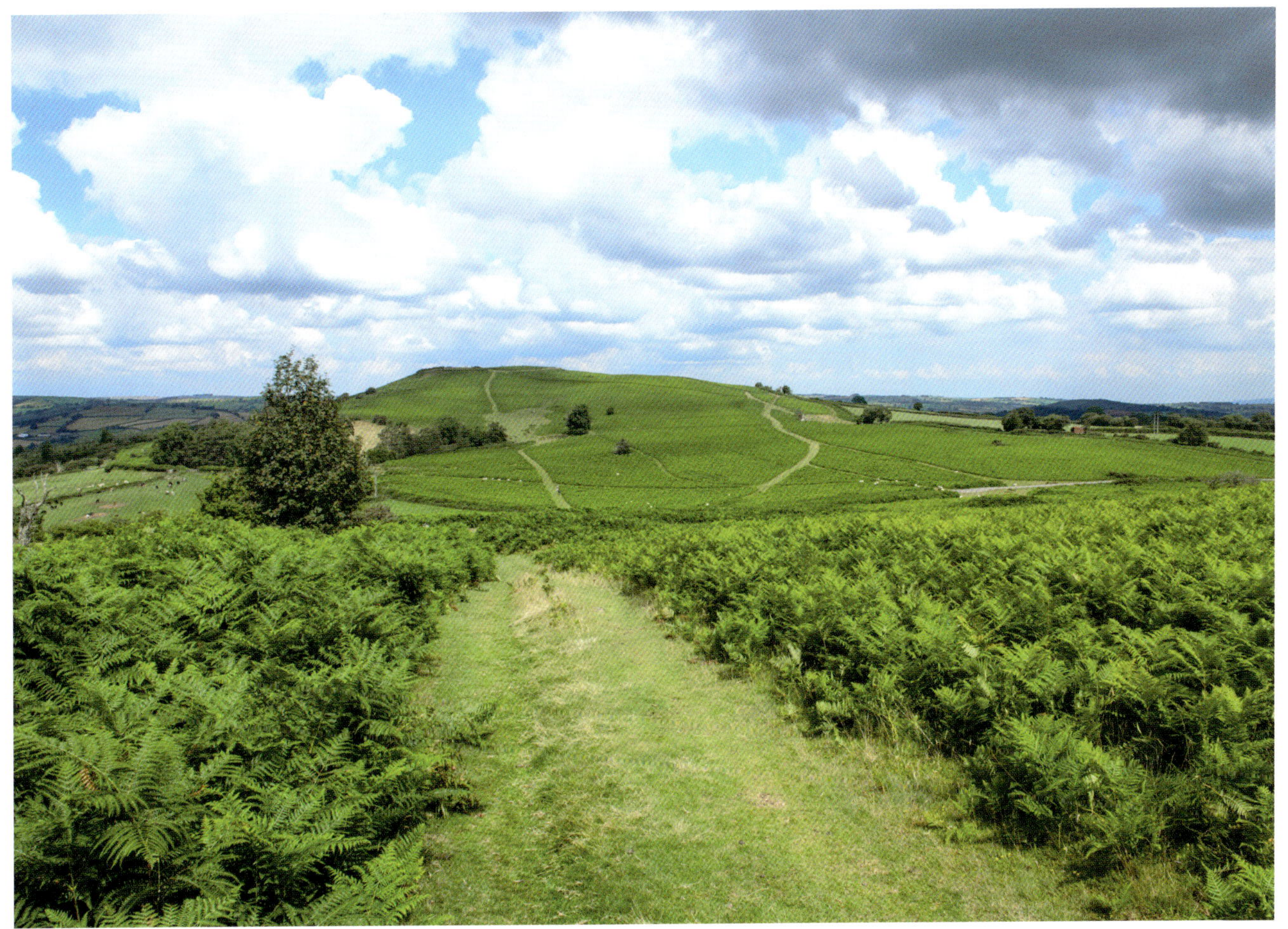

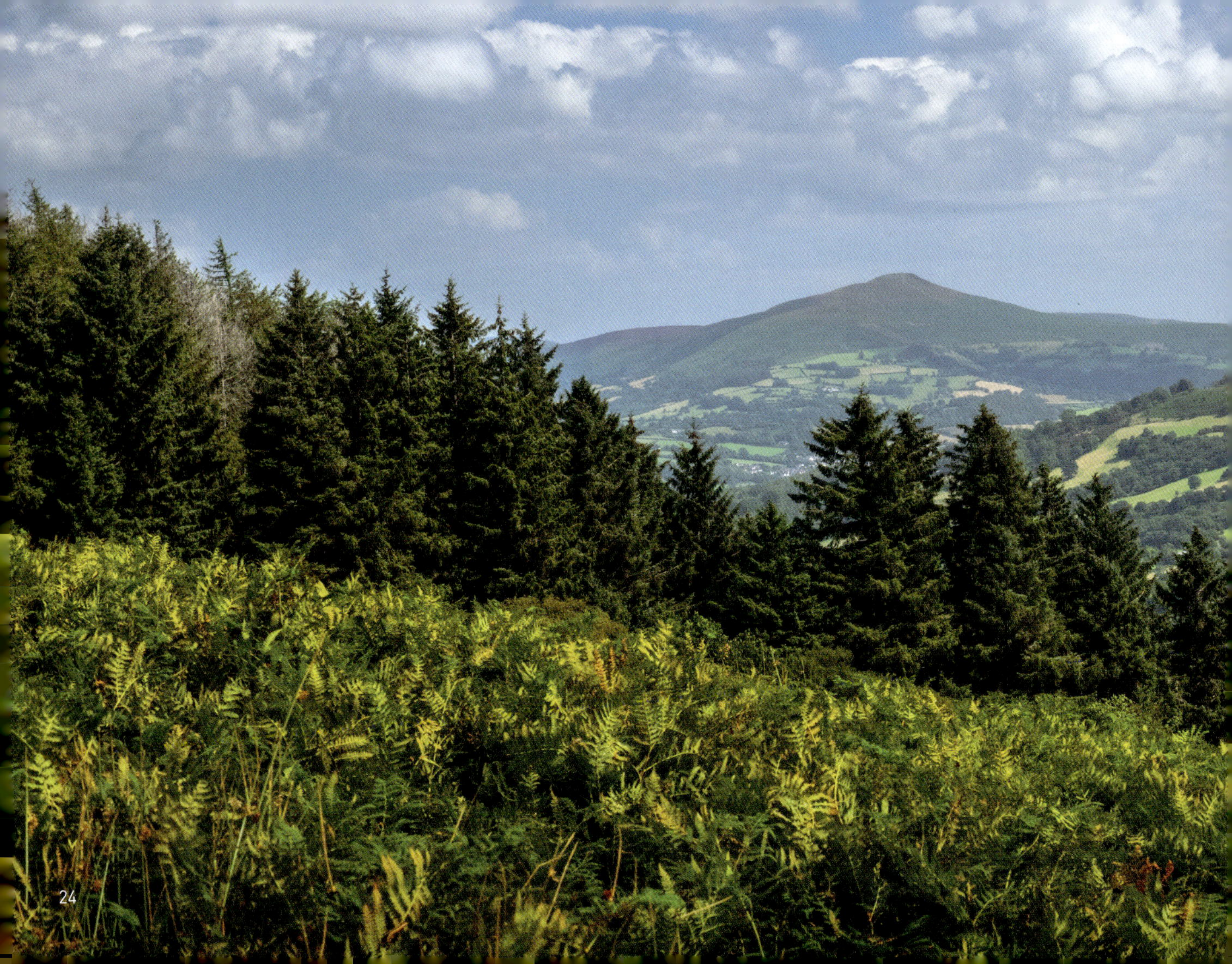

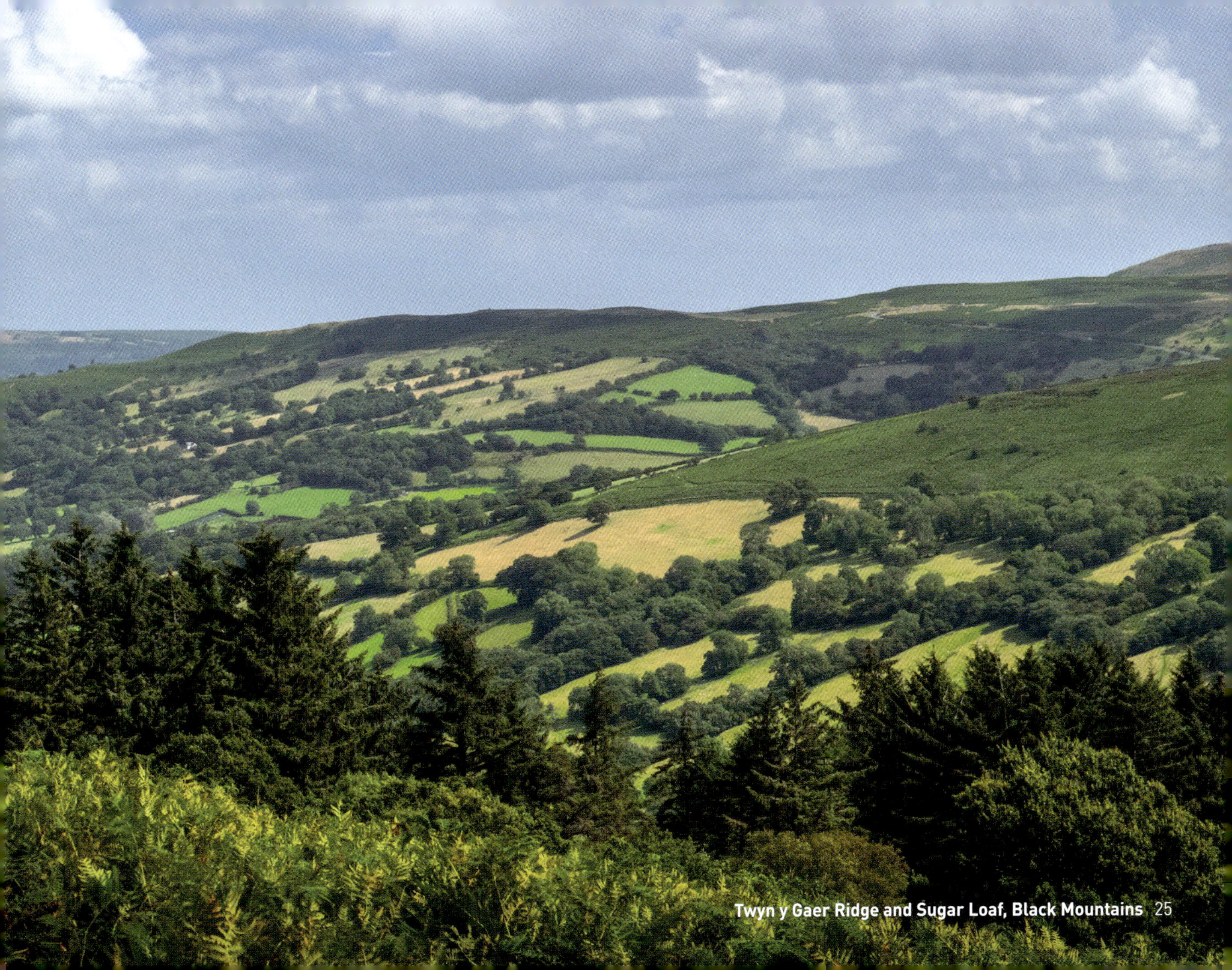

Twyn y Gaer Ridge and Sugar Loaf, Black Mountains 25

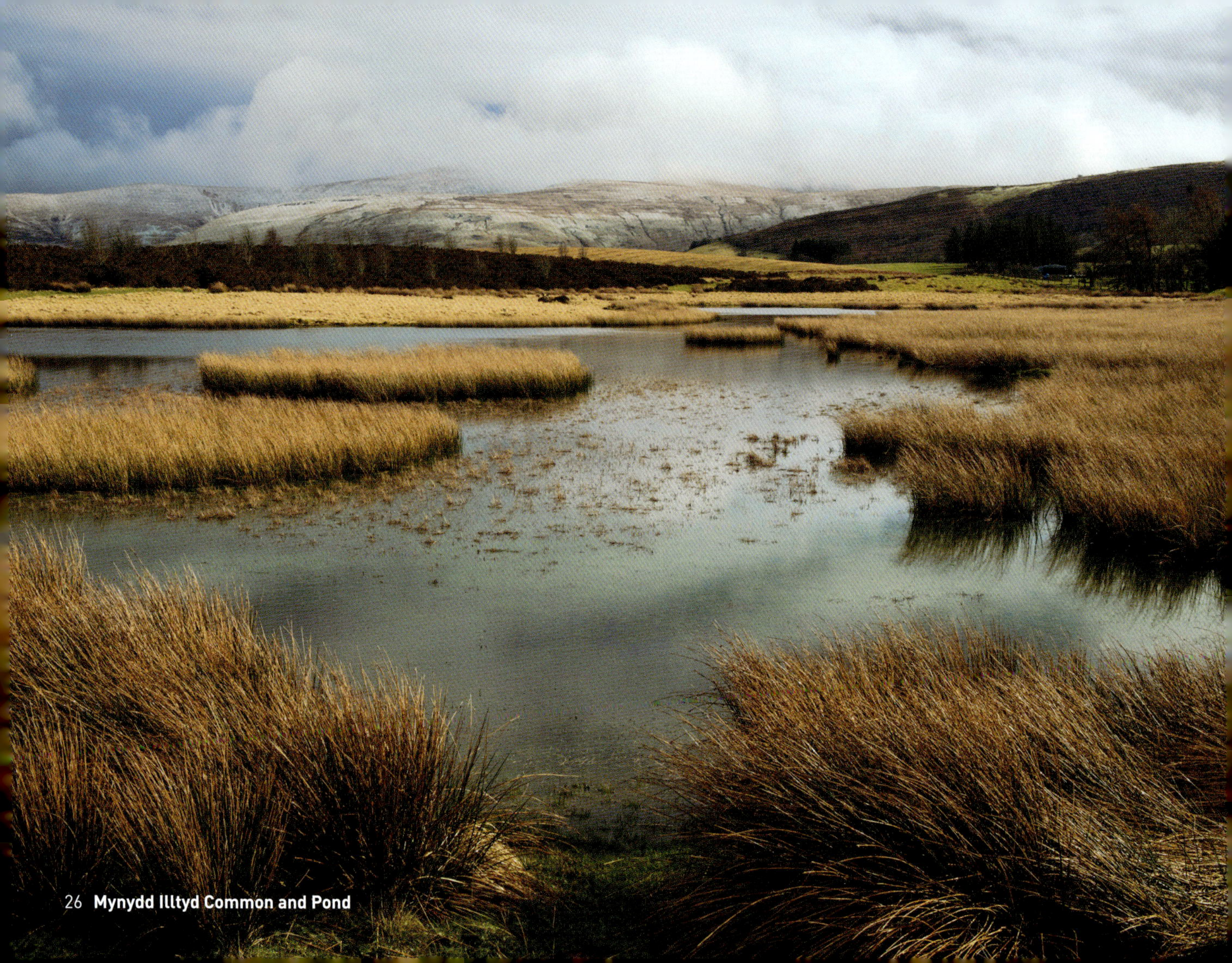

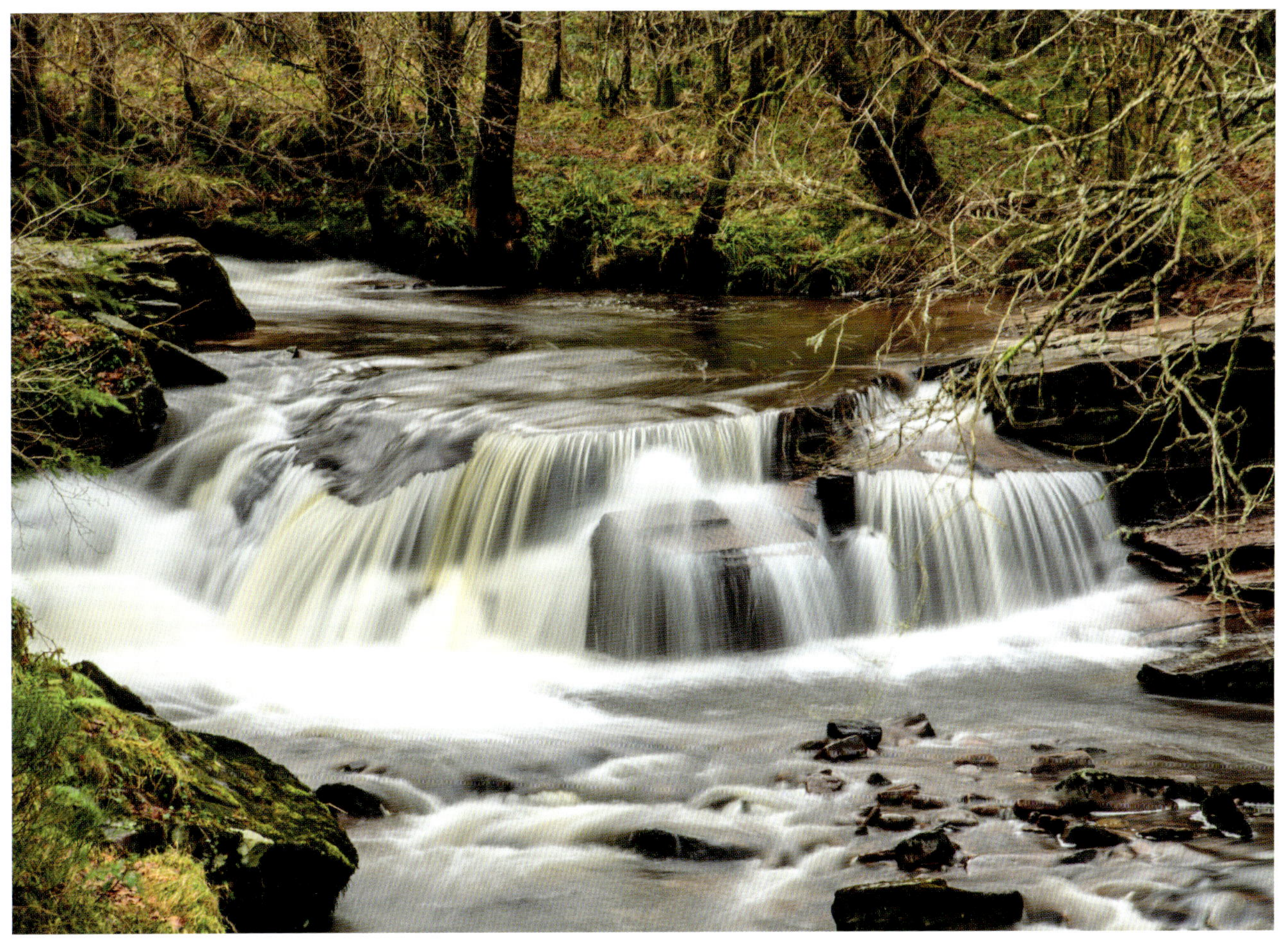

Pont Cwm y Fedwen Waterfall, Little Taff Valley 27

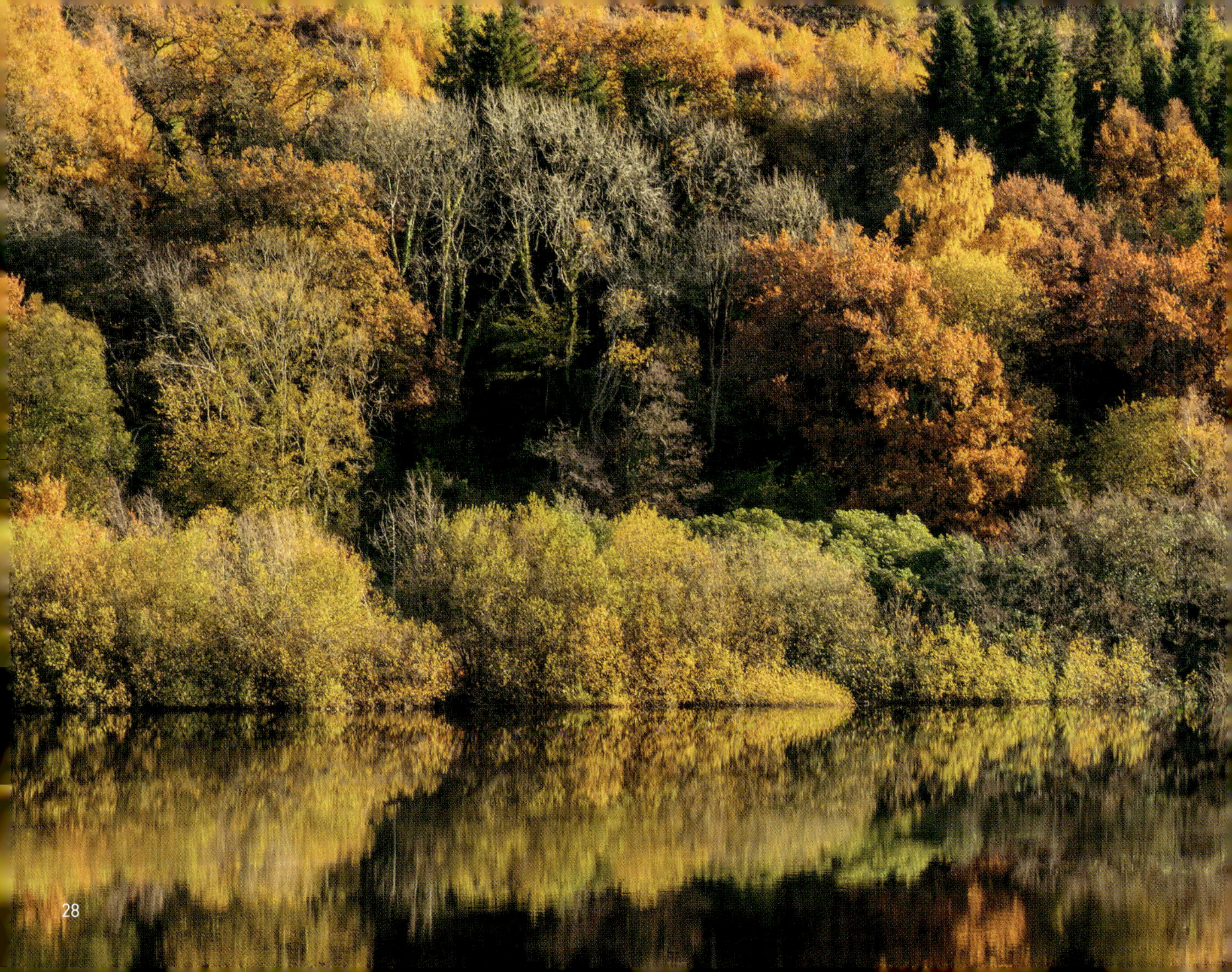

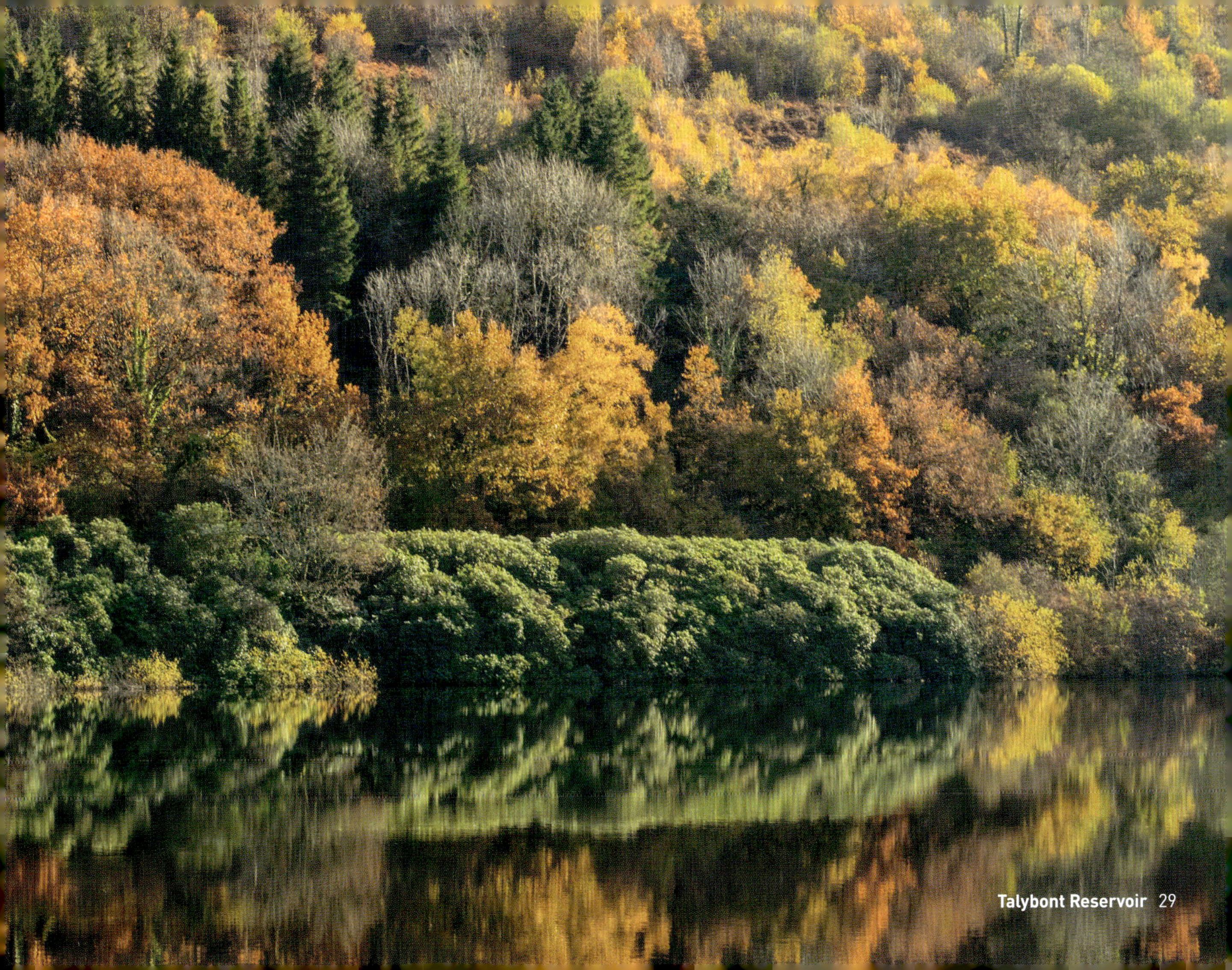
Talybont Reservoir 29

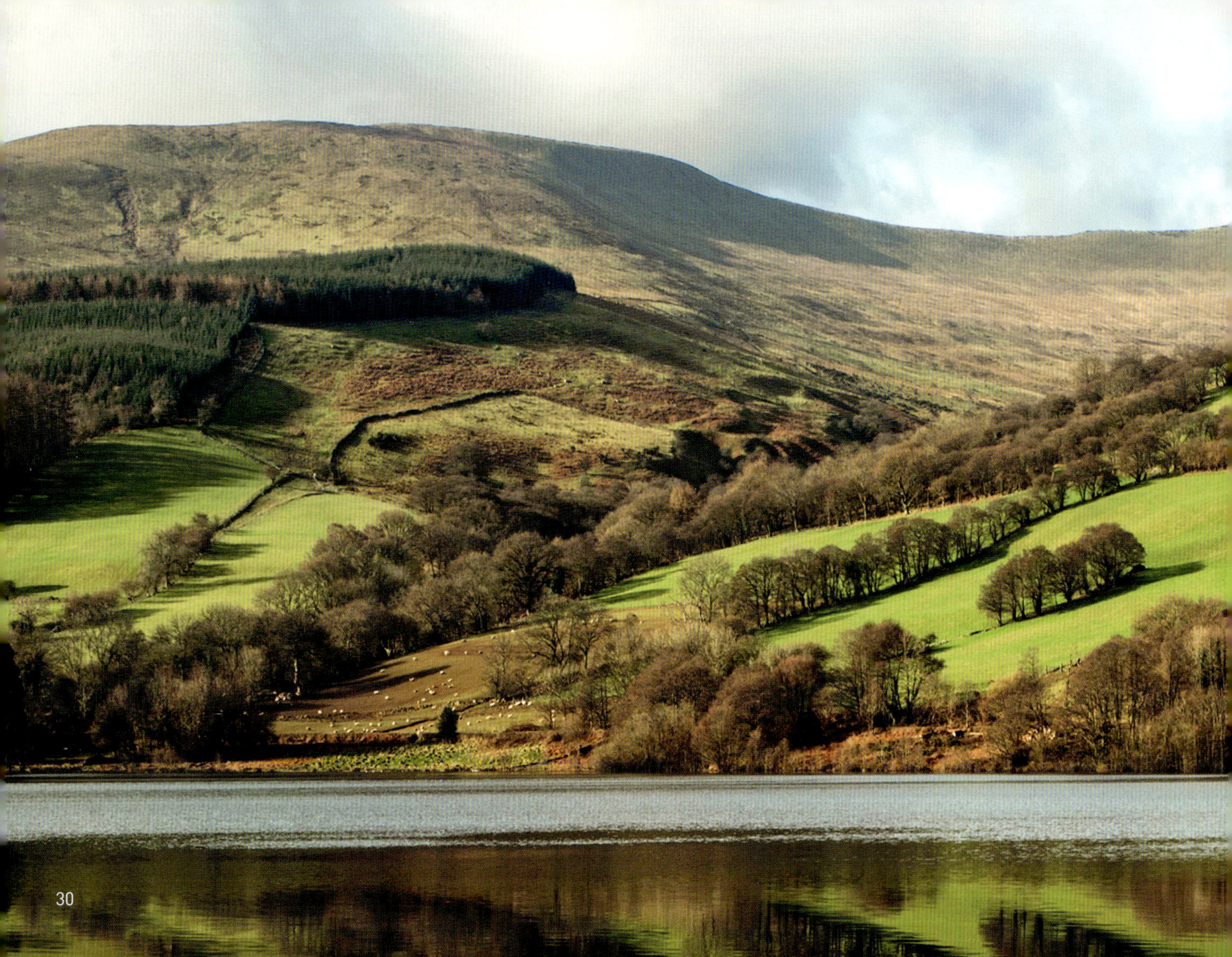

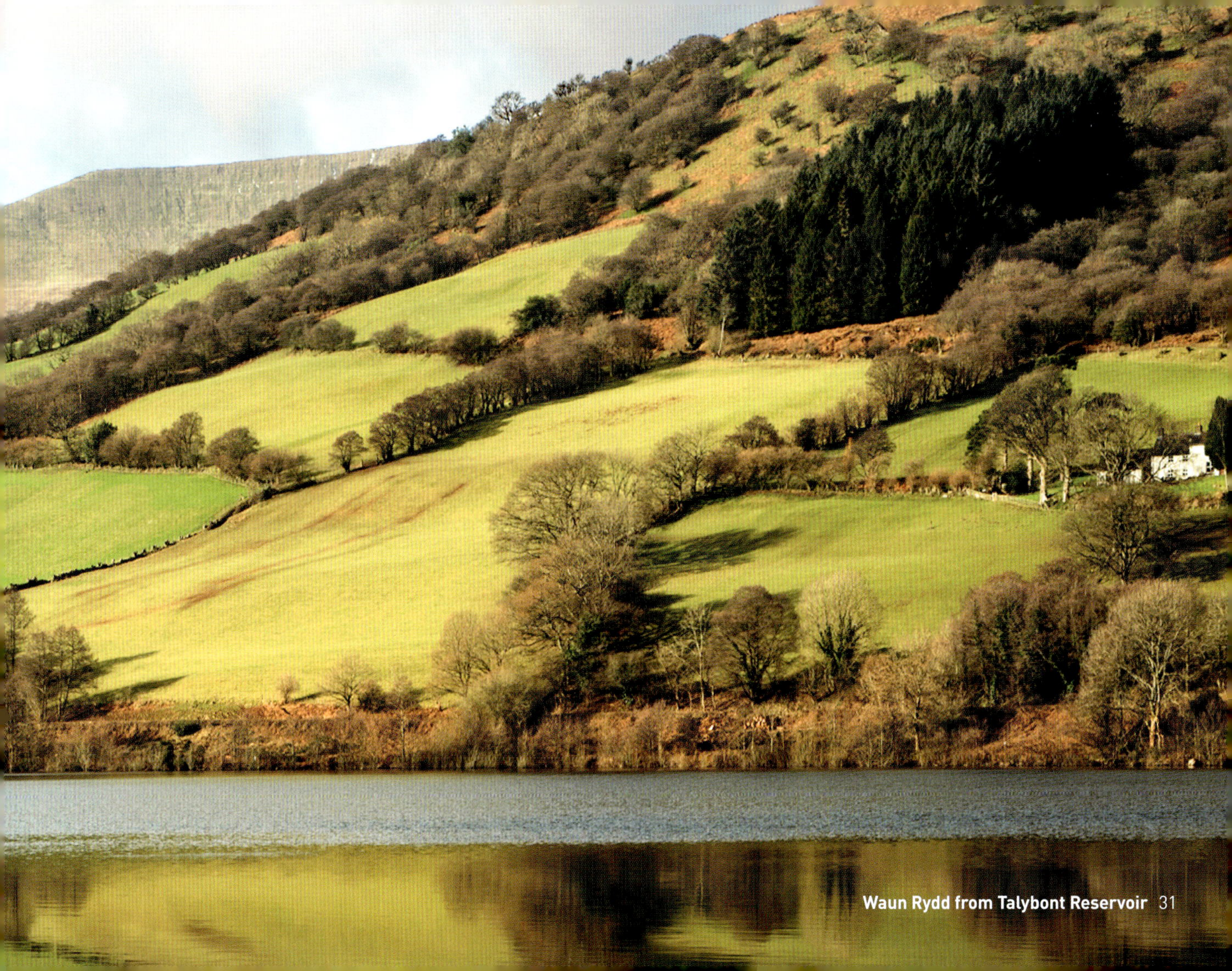

Waun Rydd from Talybont Reservoir 31

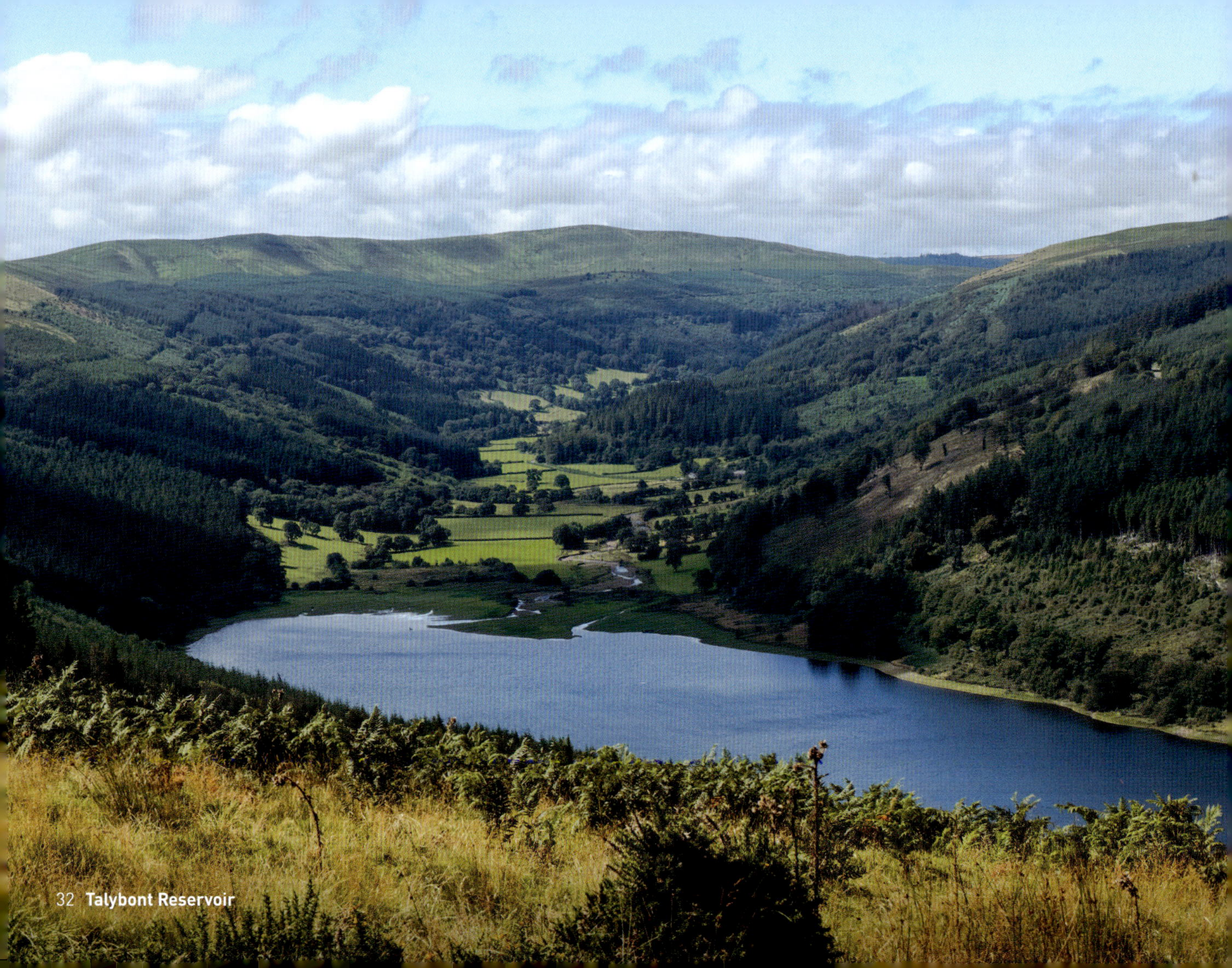

 Talybont Reservoir

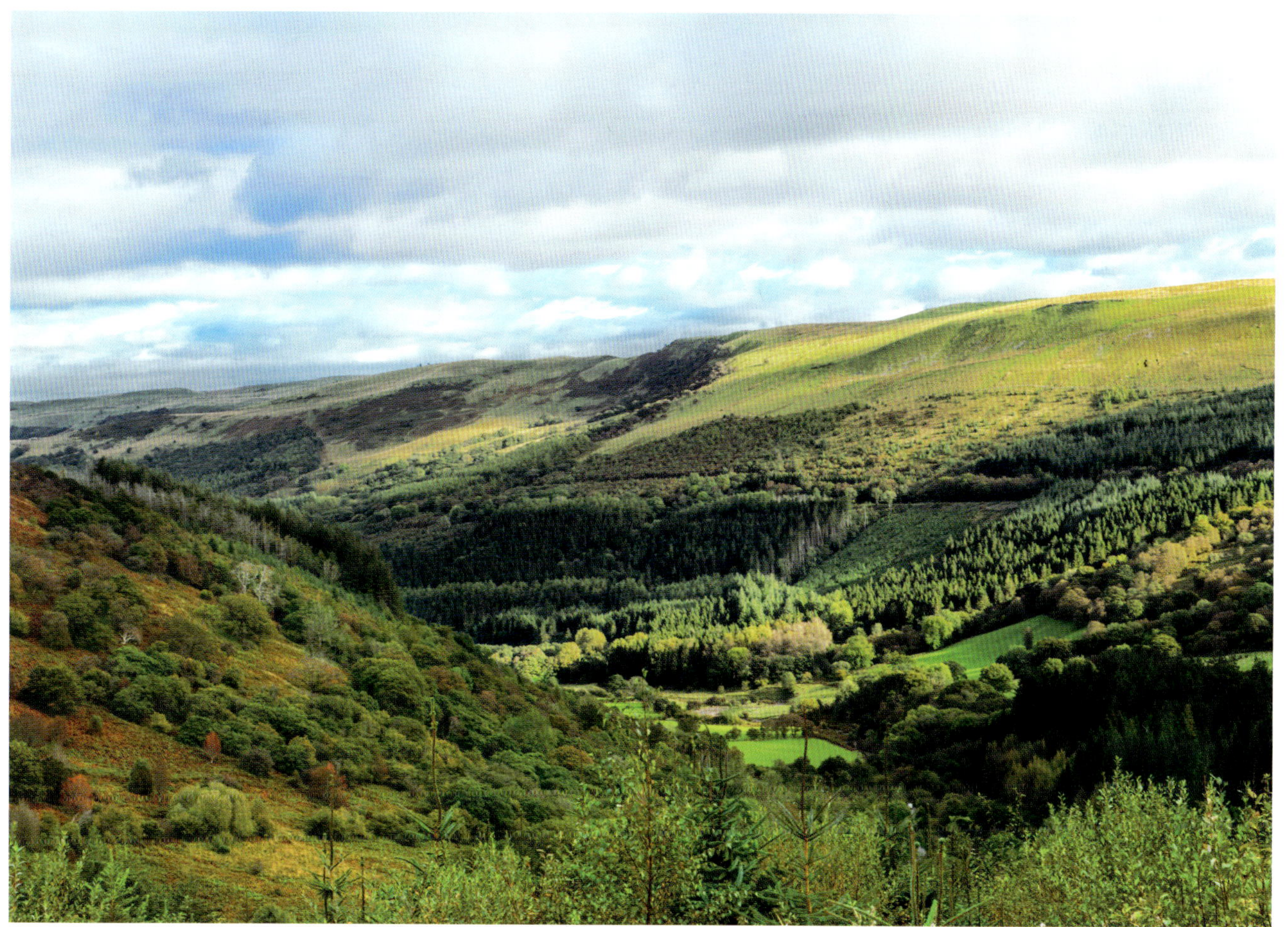

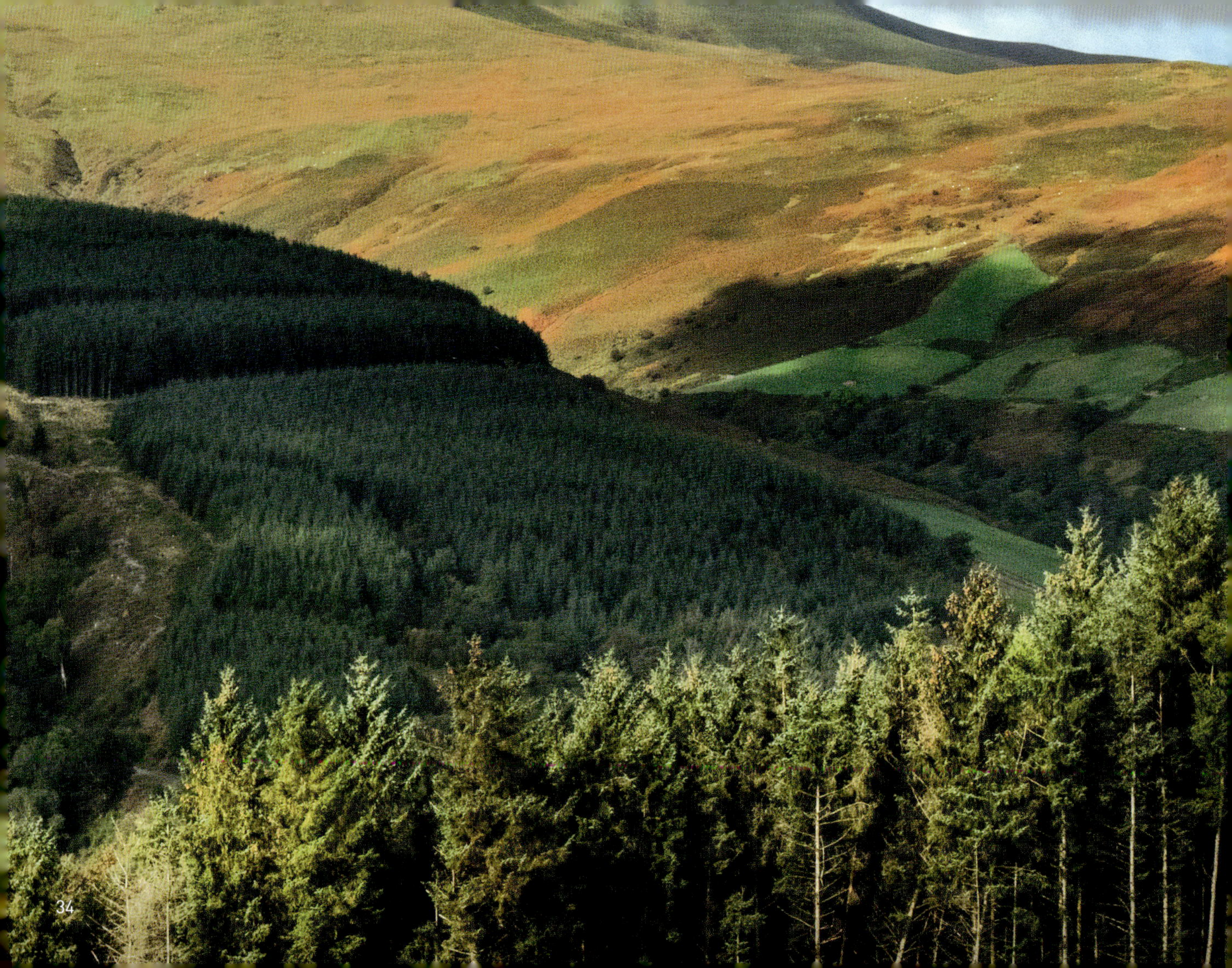

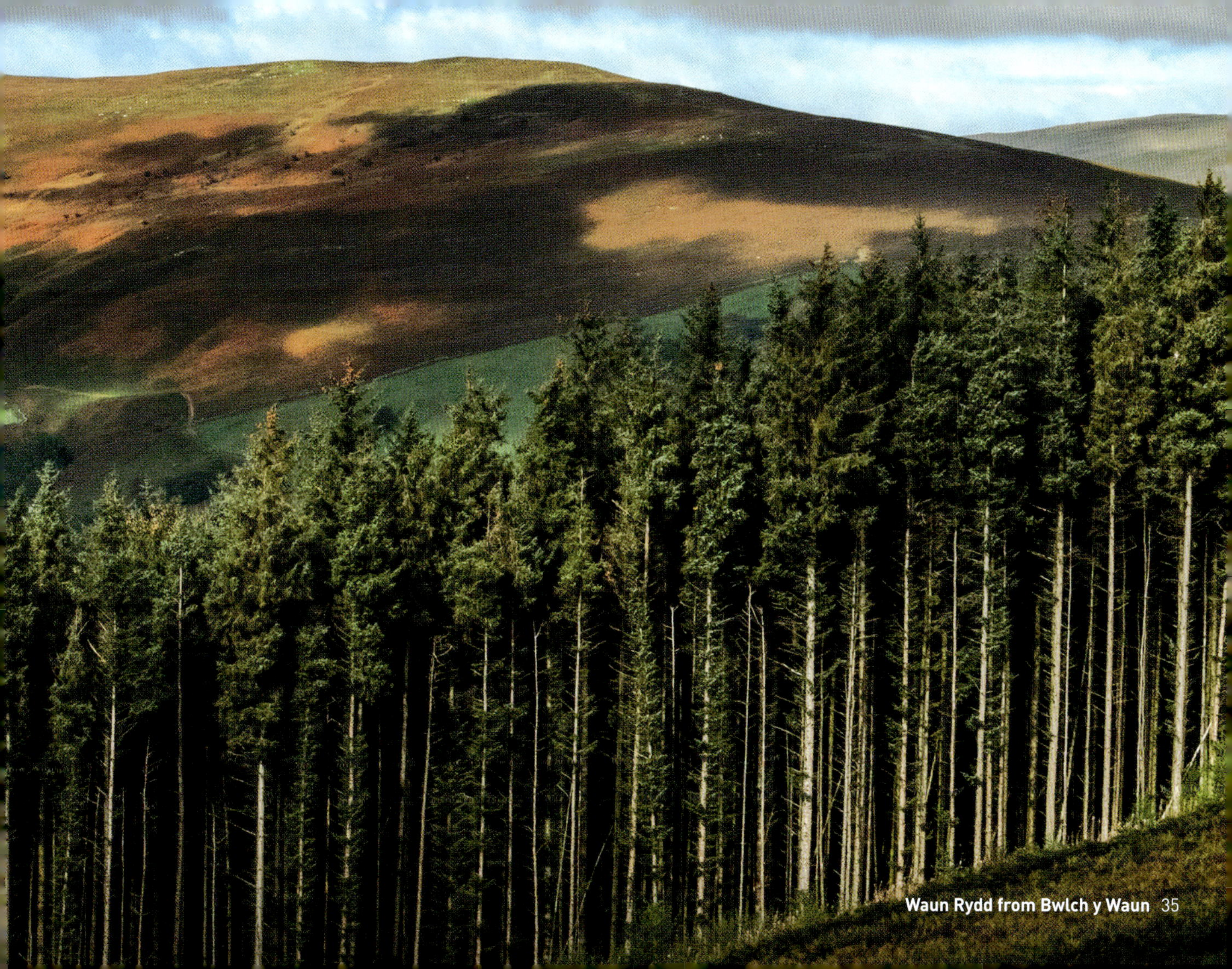
Waun Rydd from Bwlch y Waun 35

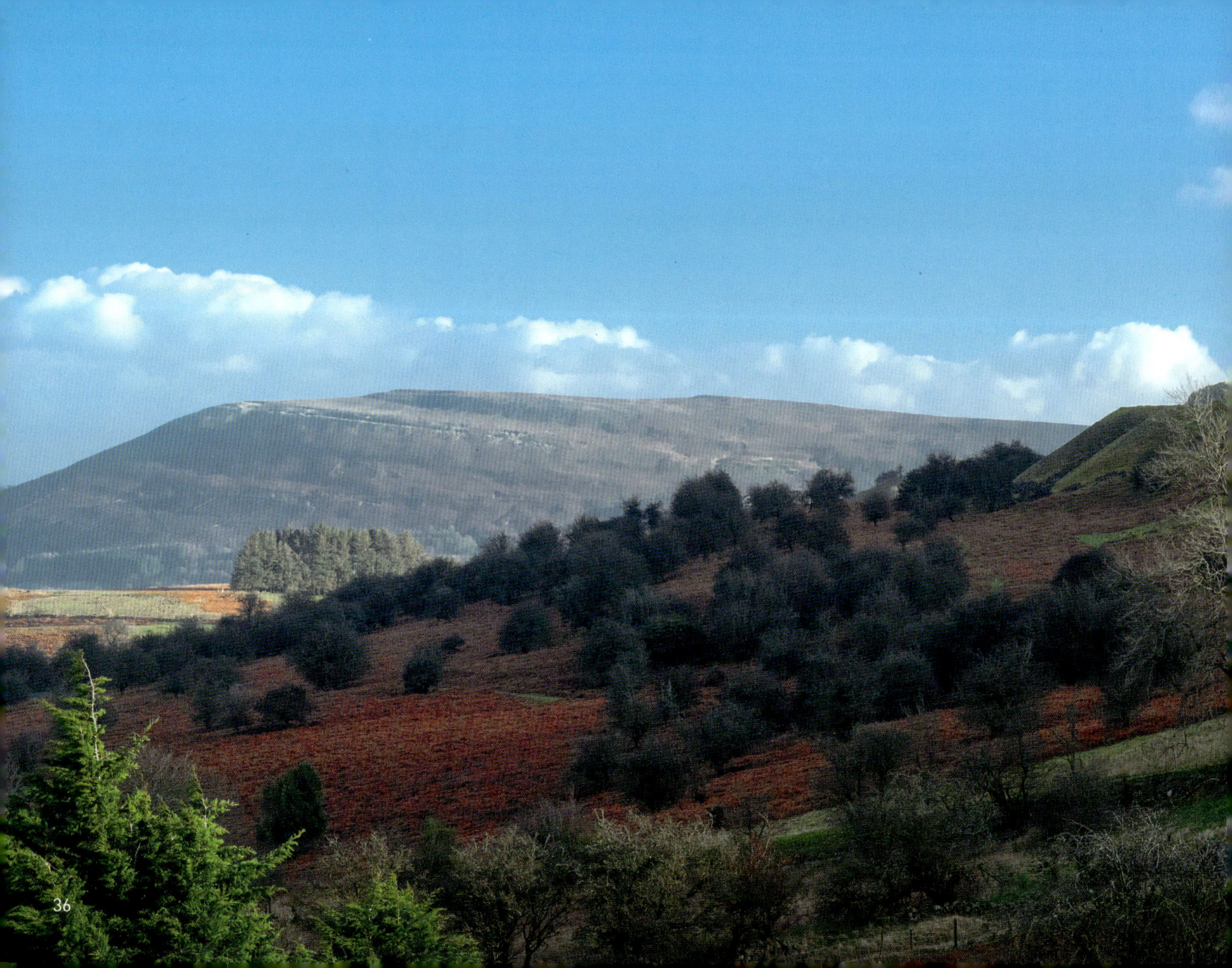

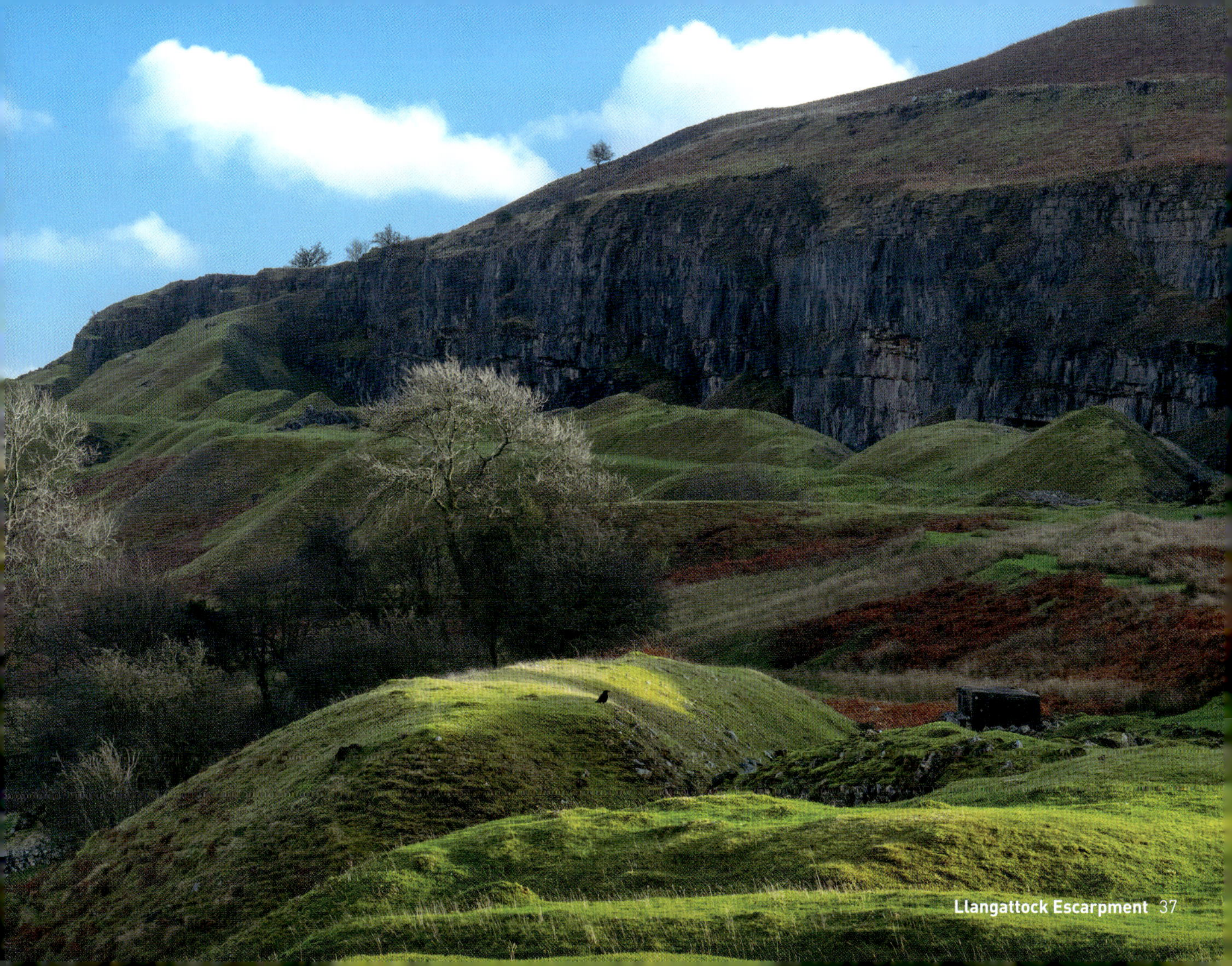
Llangattock Escarpment 37

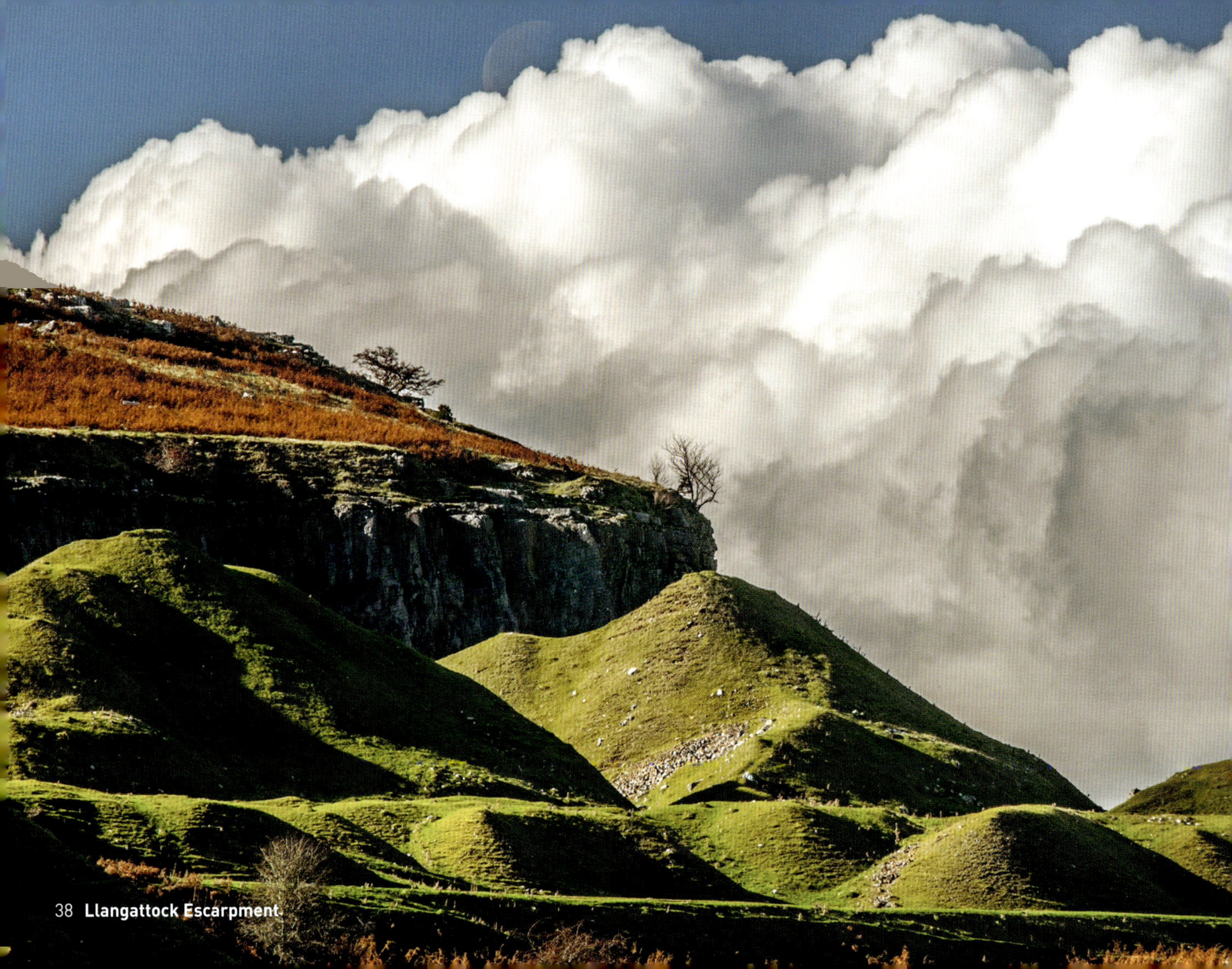

38 Llangattock Escarpment

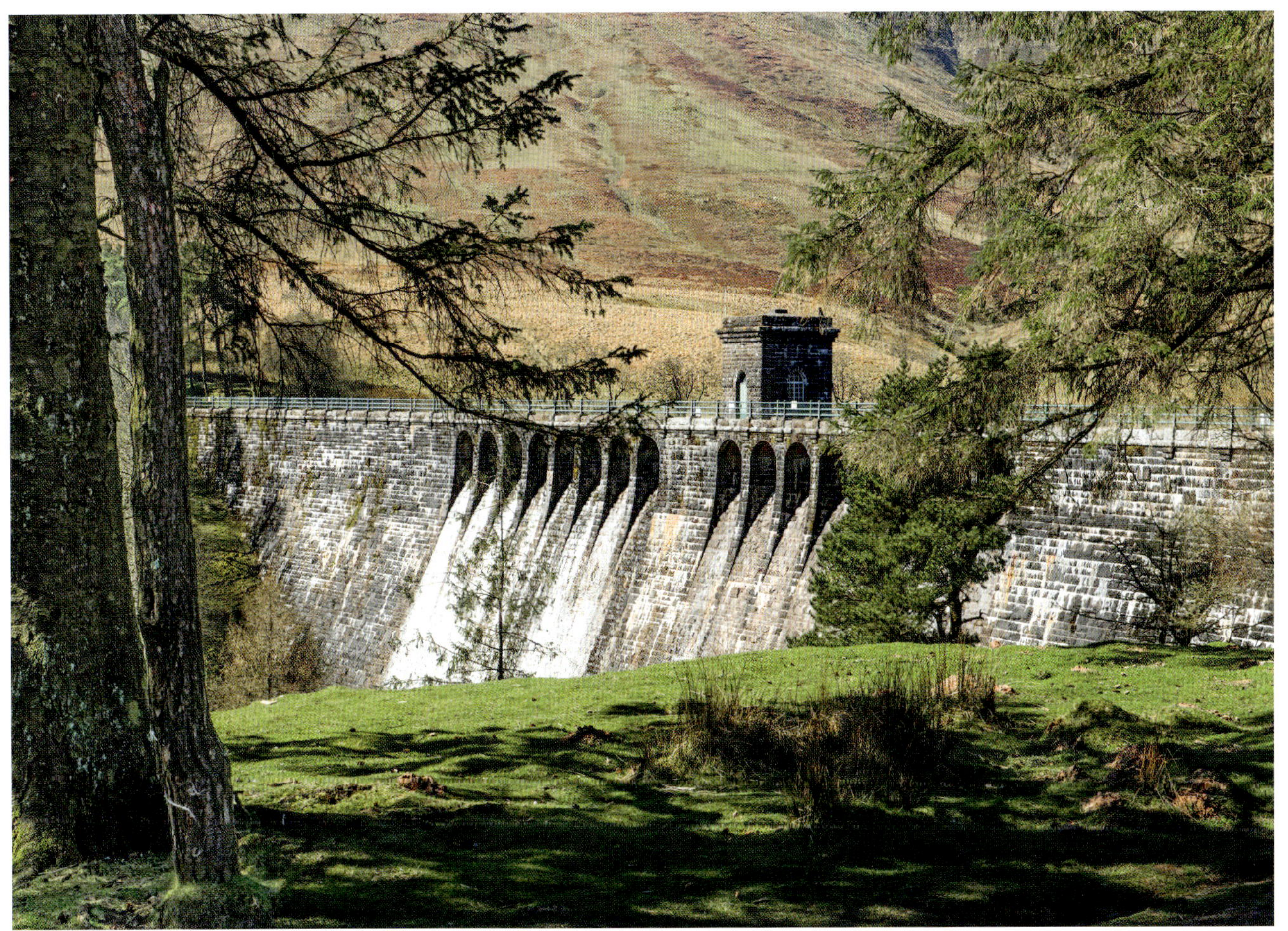

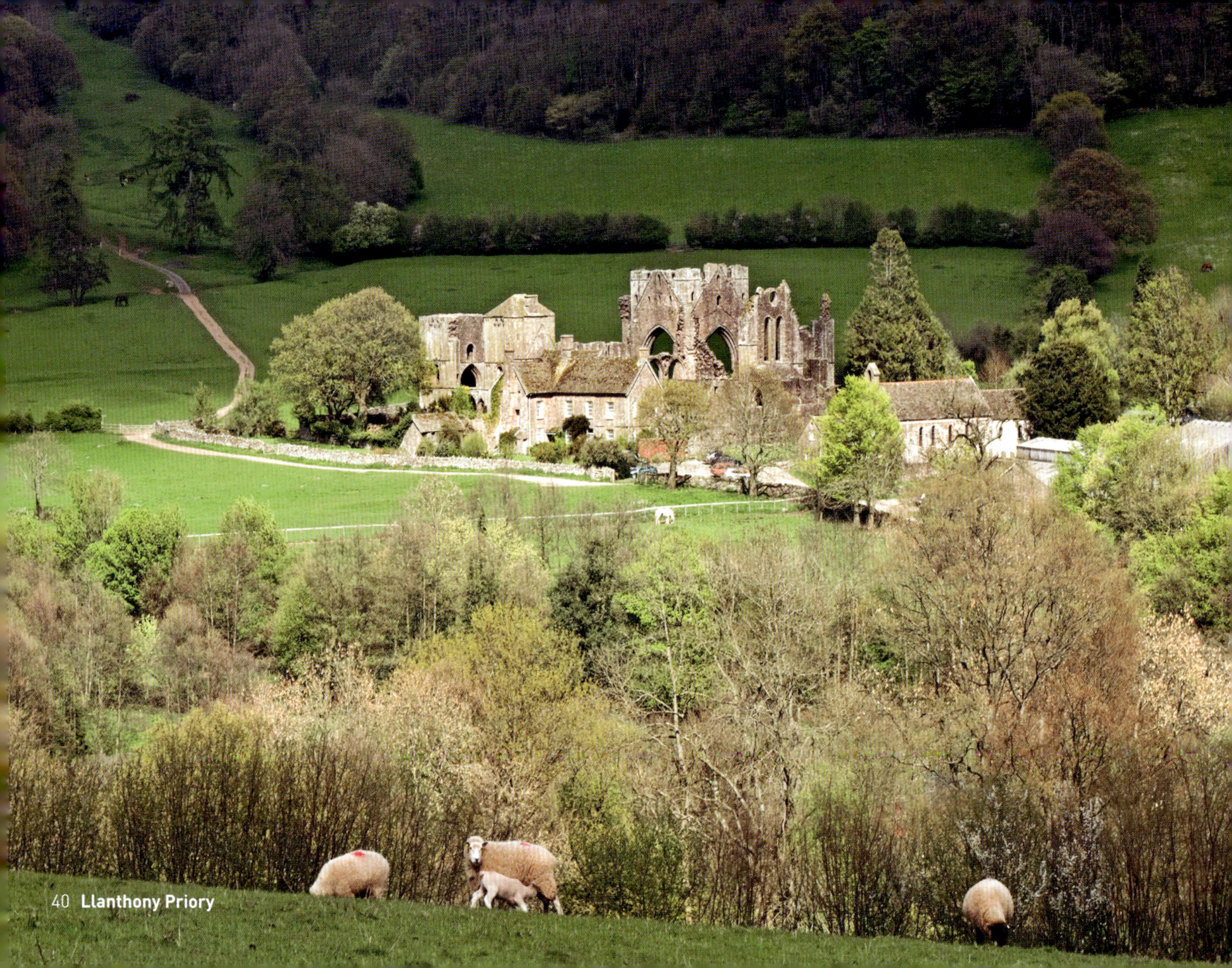

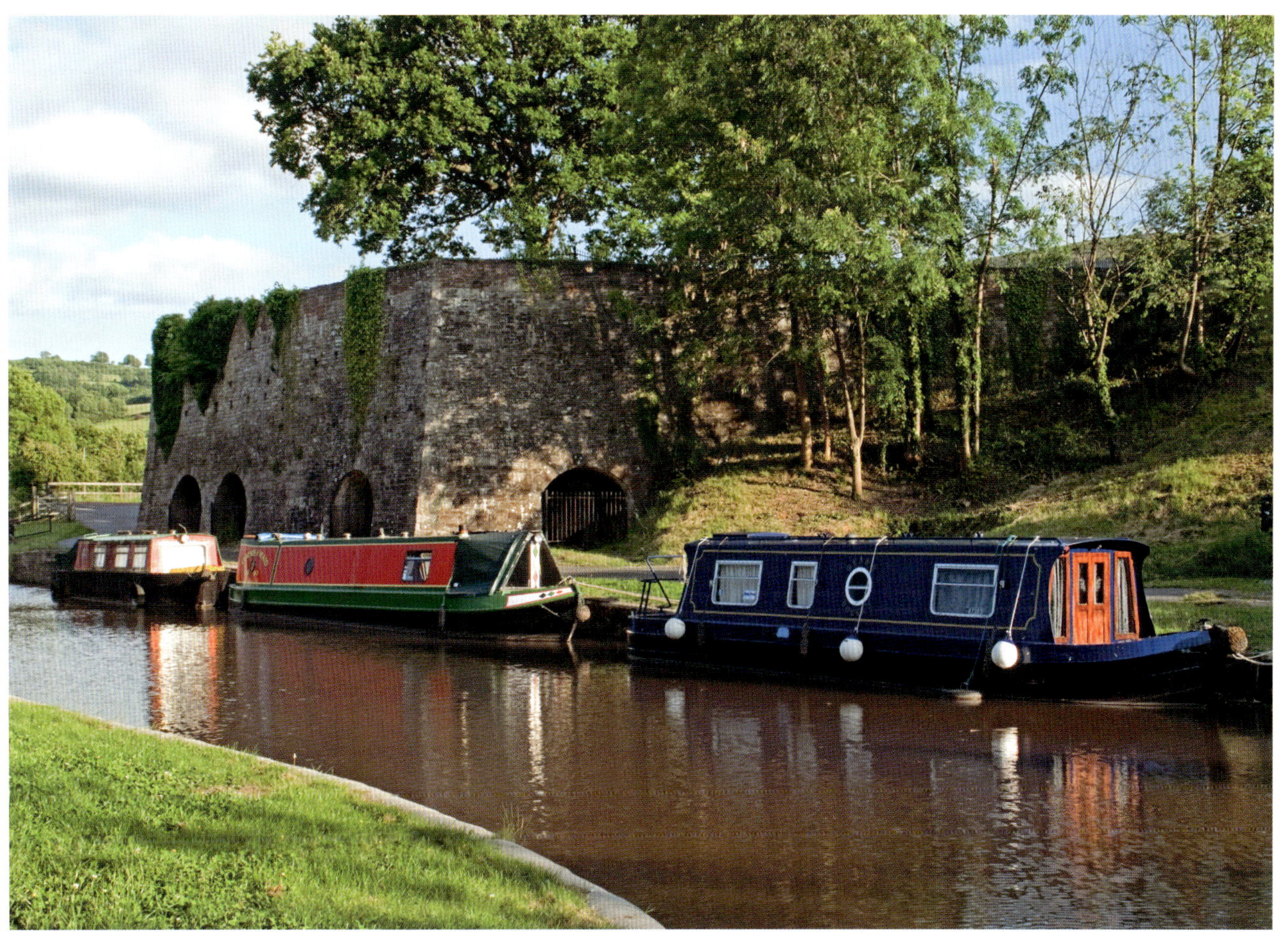

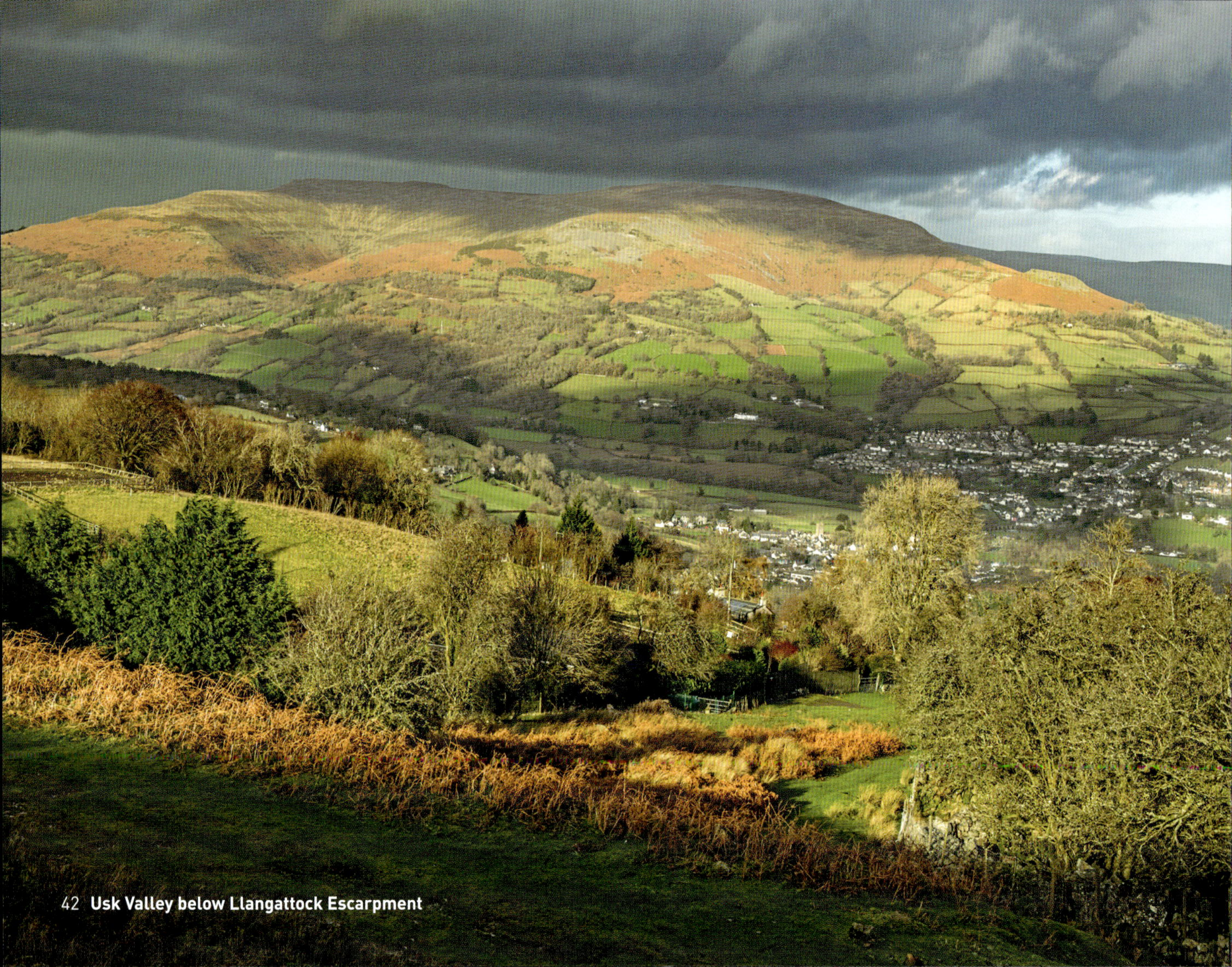

 Usk Valley below Llangattock Escarpment

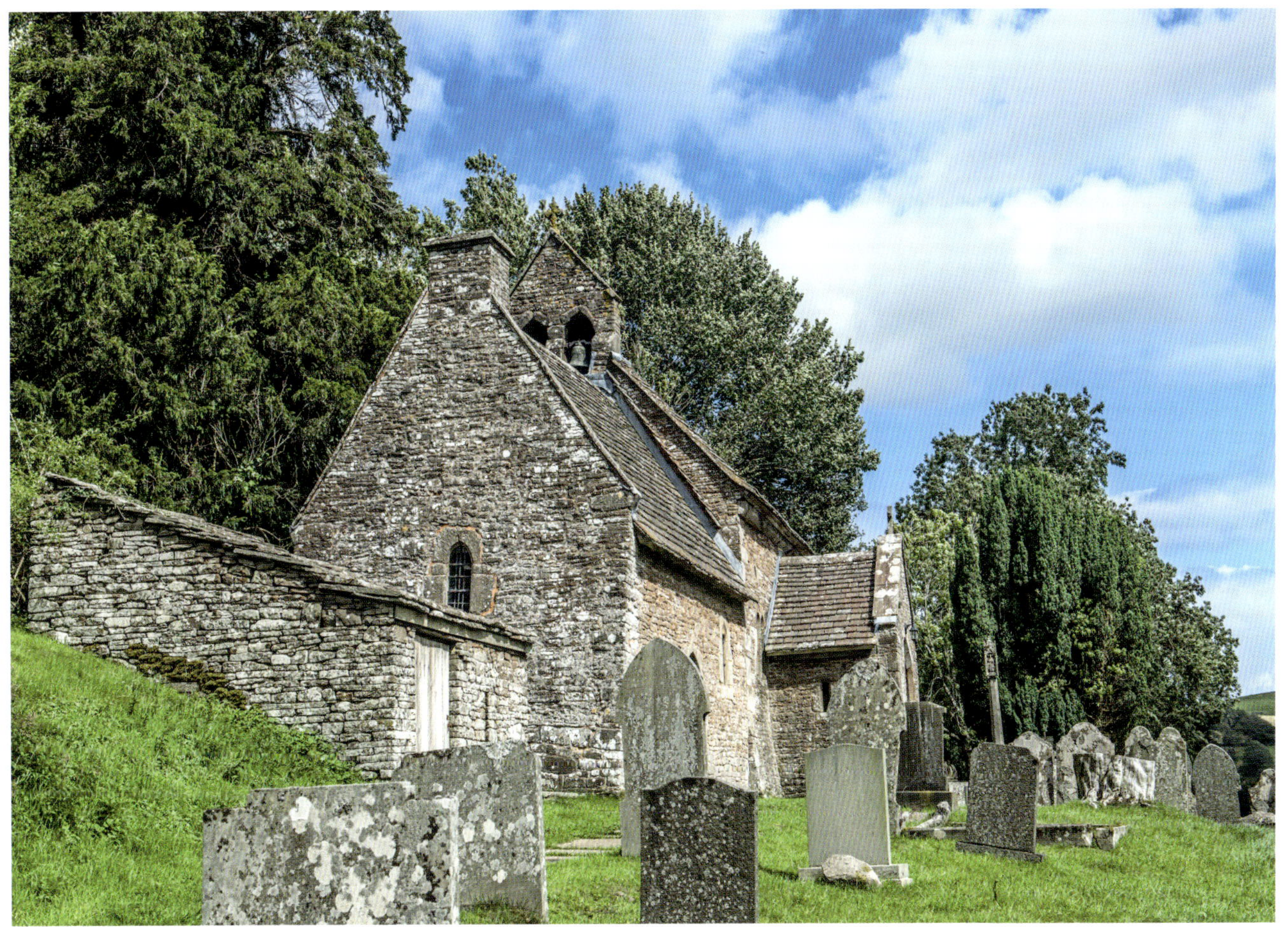

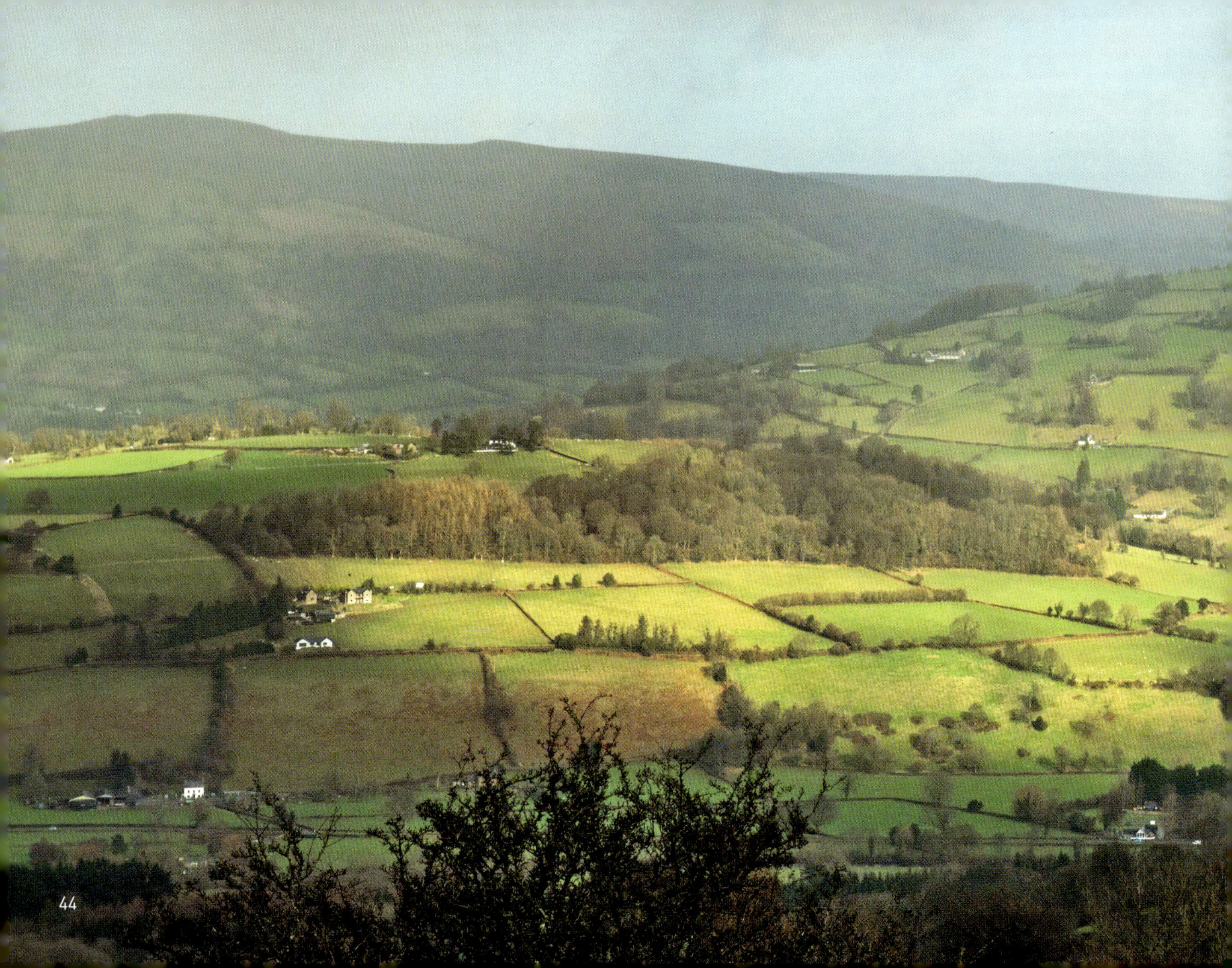

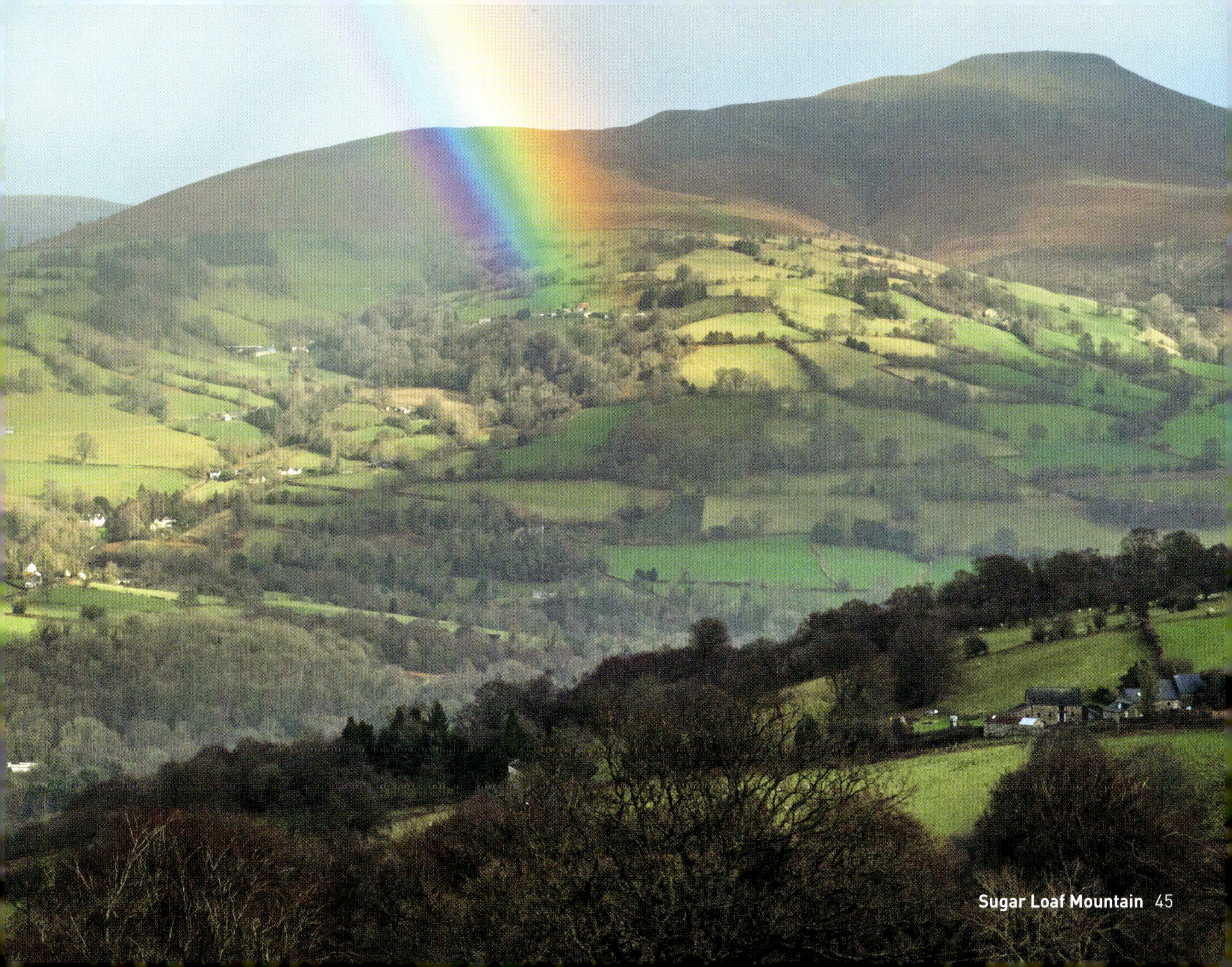

Sugar Loaf Mountain 45

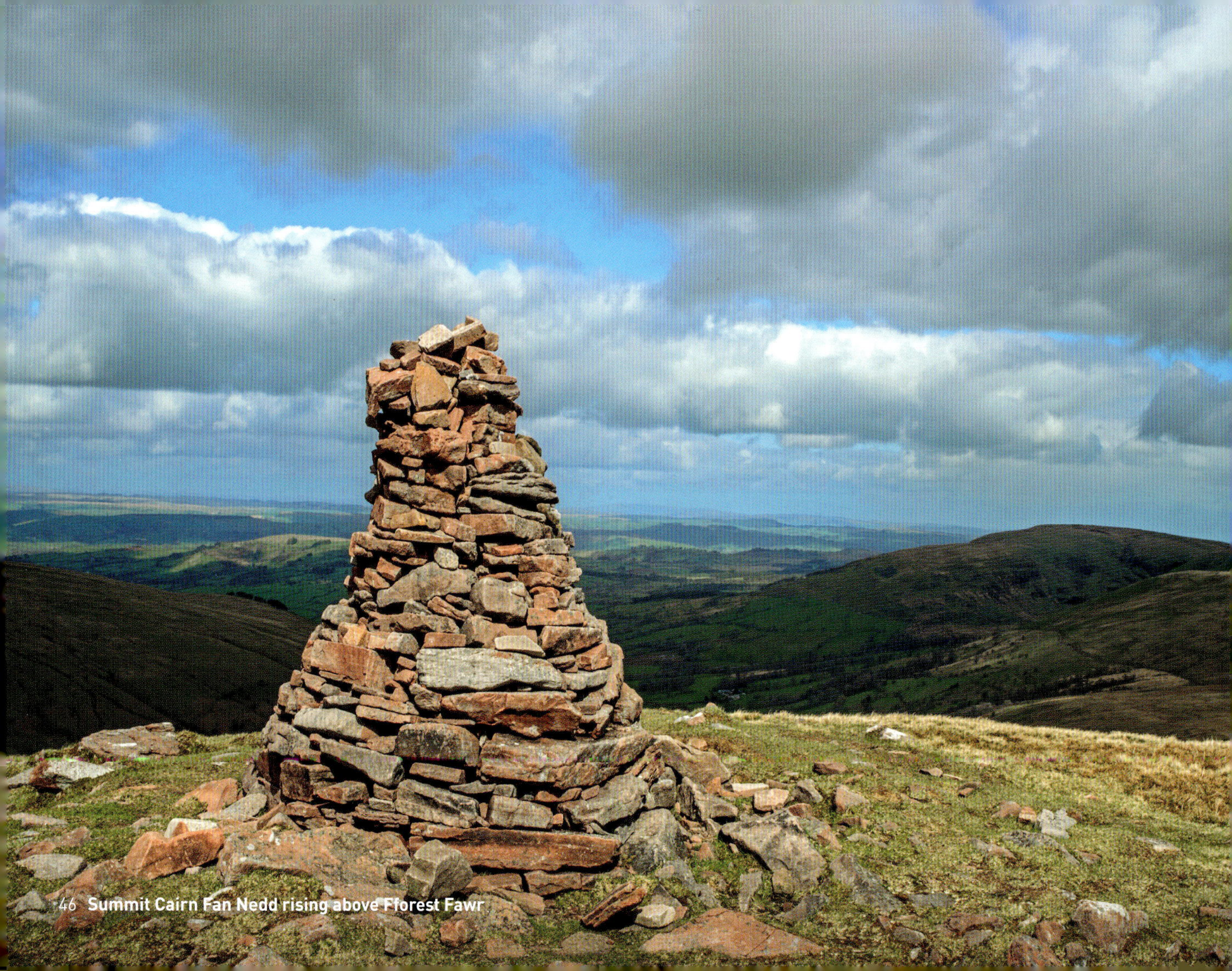

 Summit Cairn Fan Nedd rising above Fforest Fawr

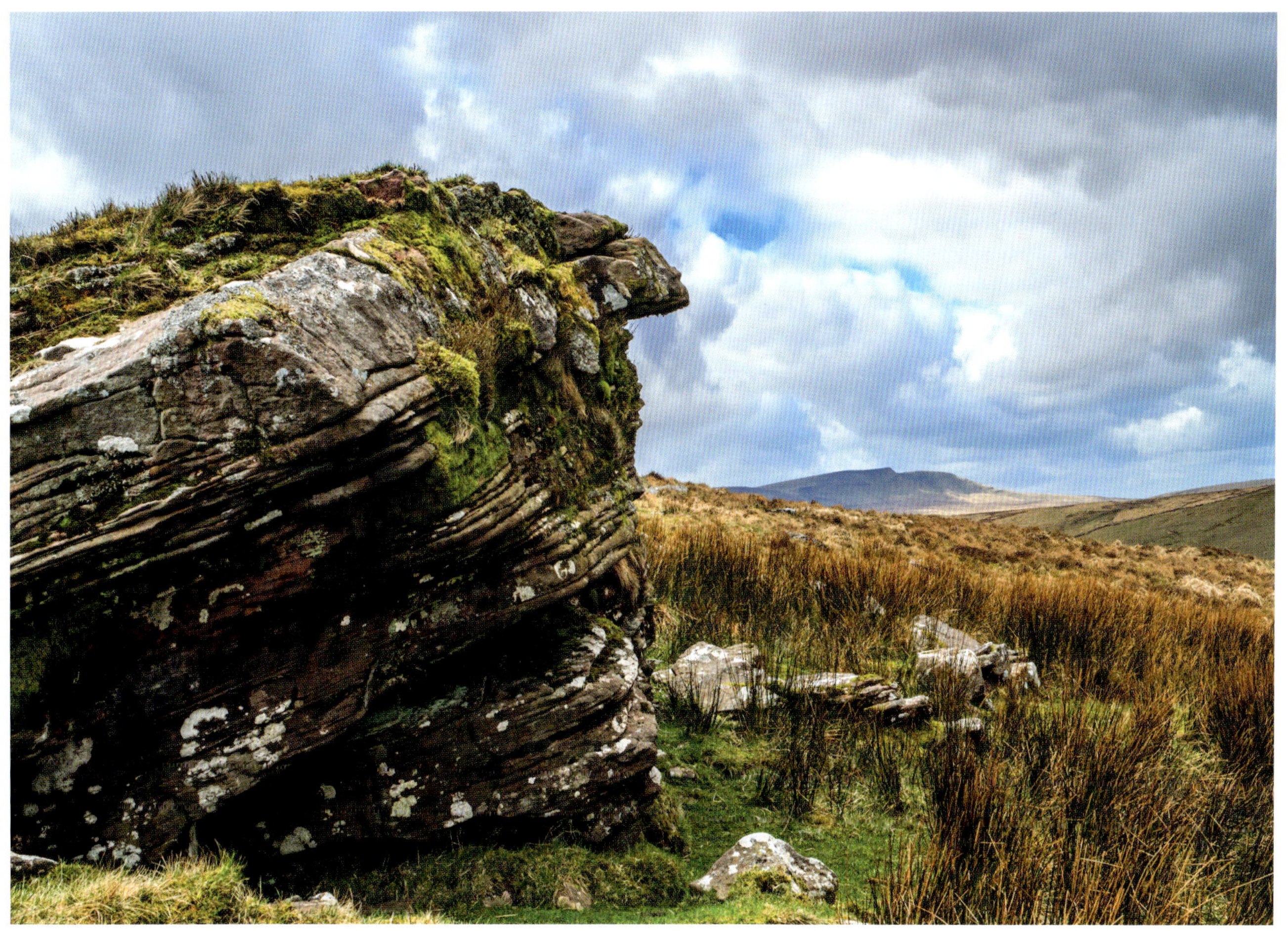

Fan Nedd Fforest Fawr towards Pen y Fan and Corn Du

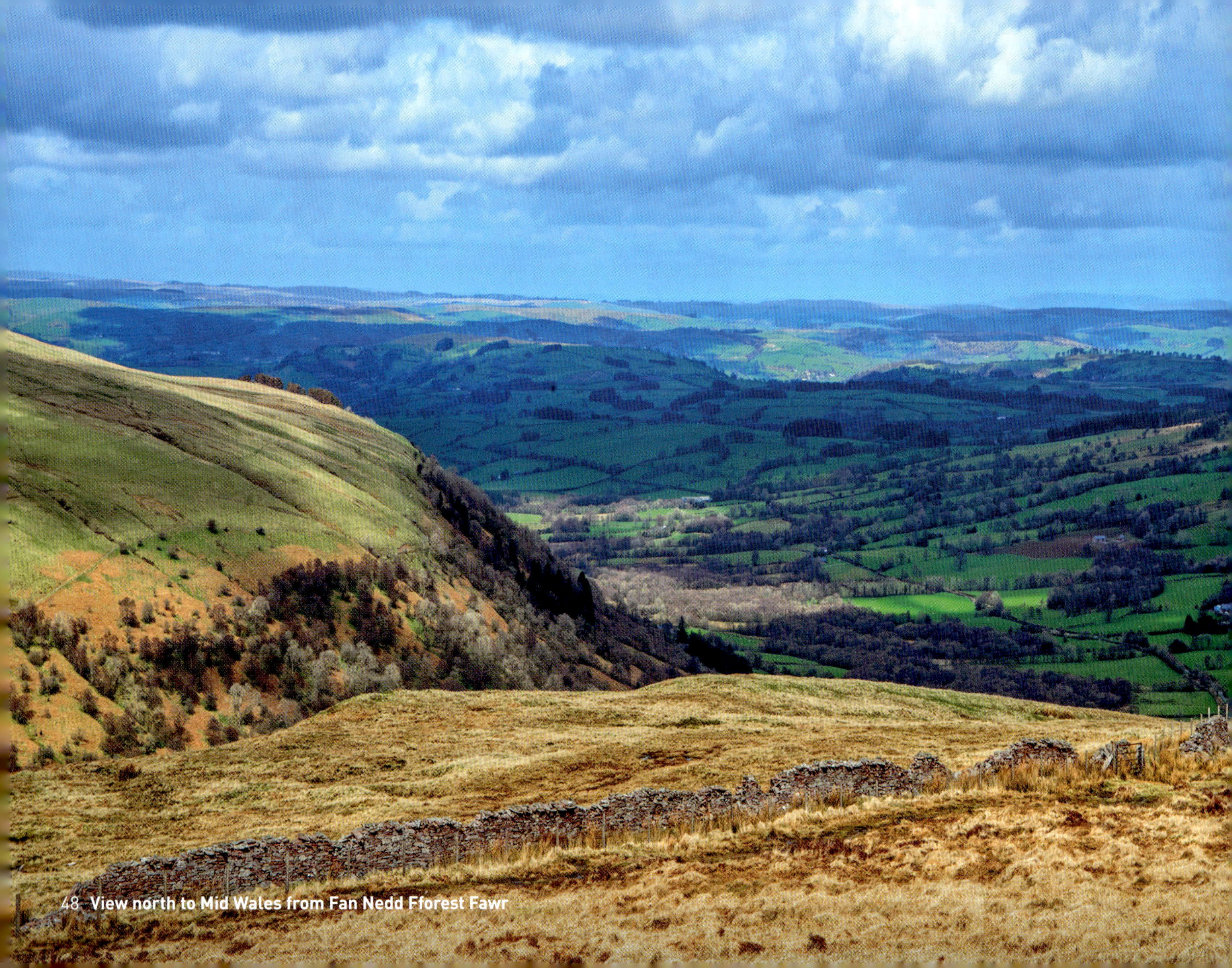

48 View north to Mid Wales from Fan Nedd Fforest Fawr

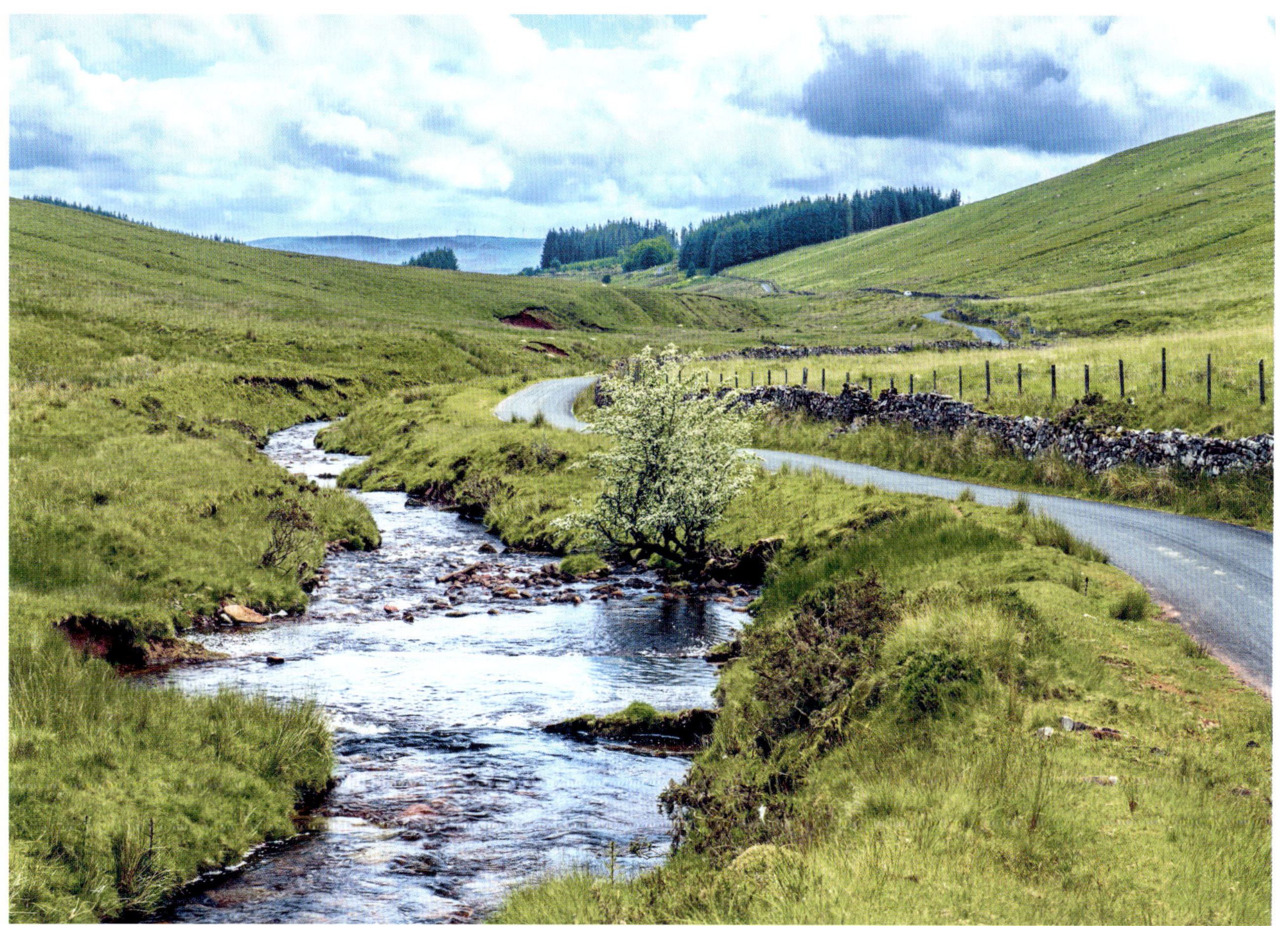

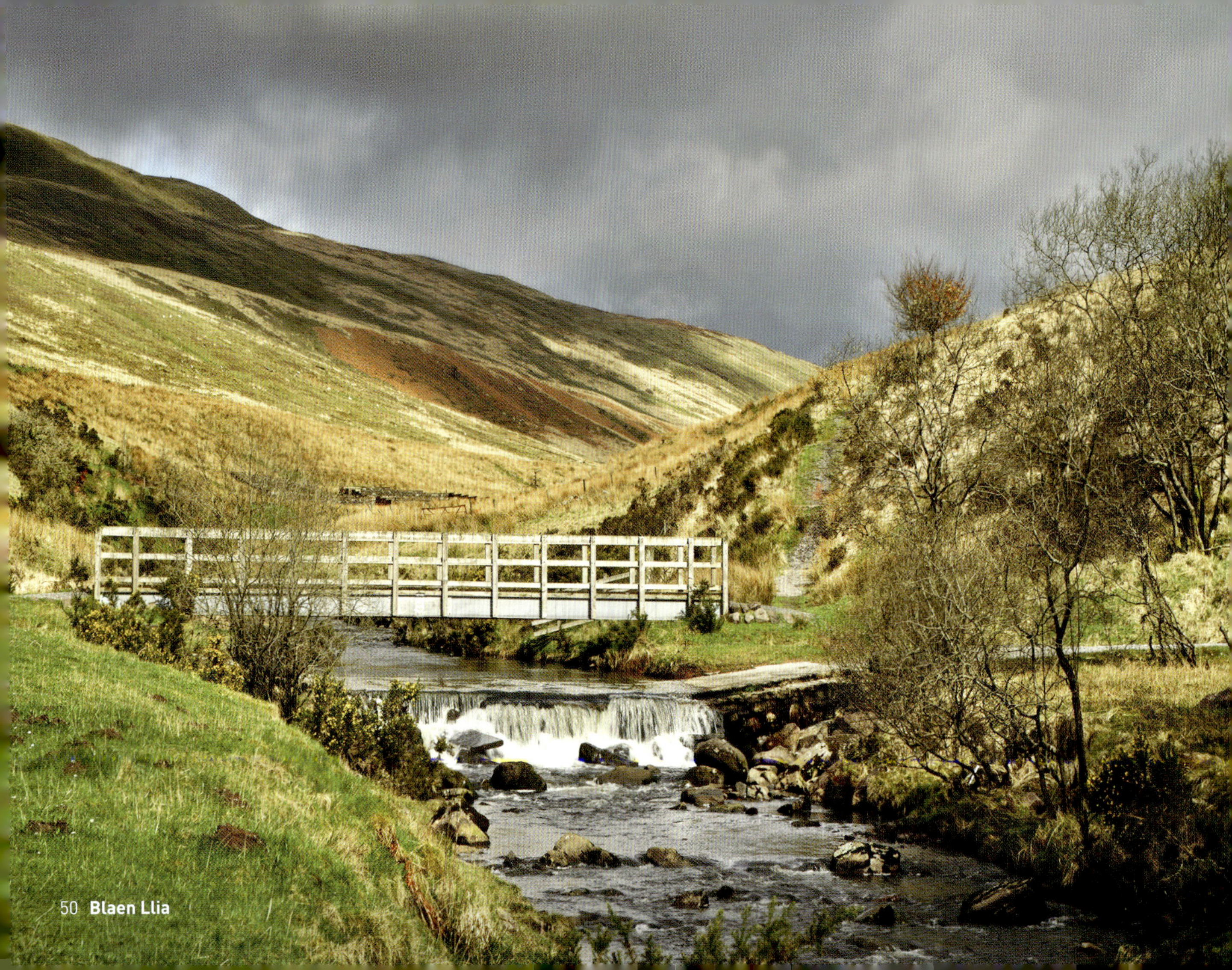

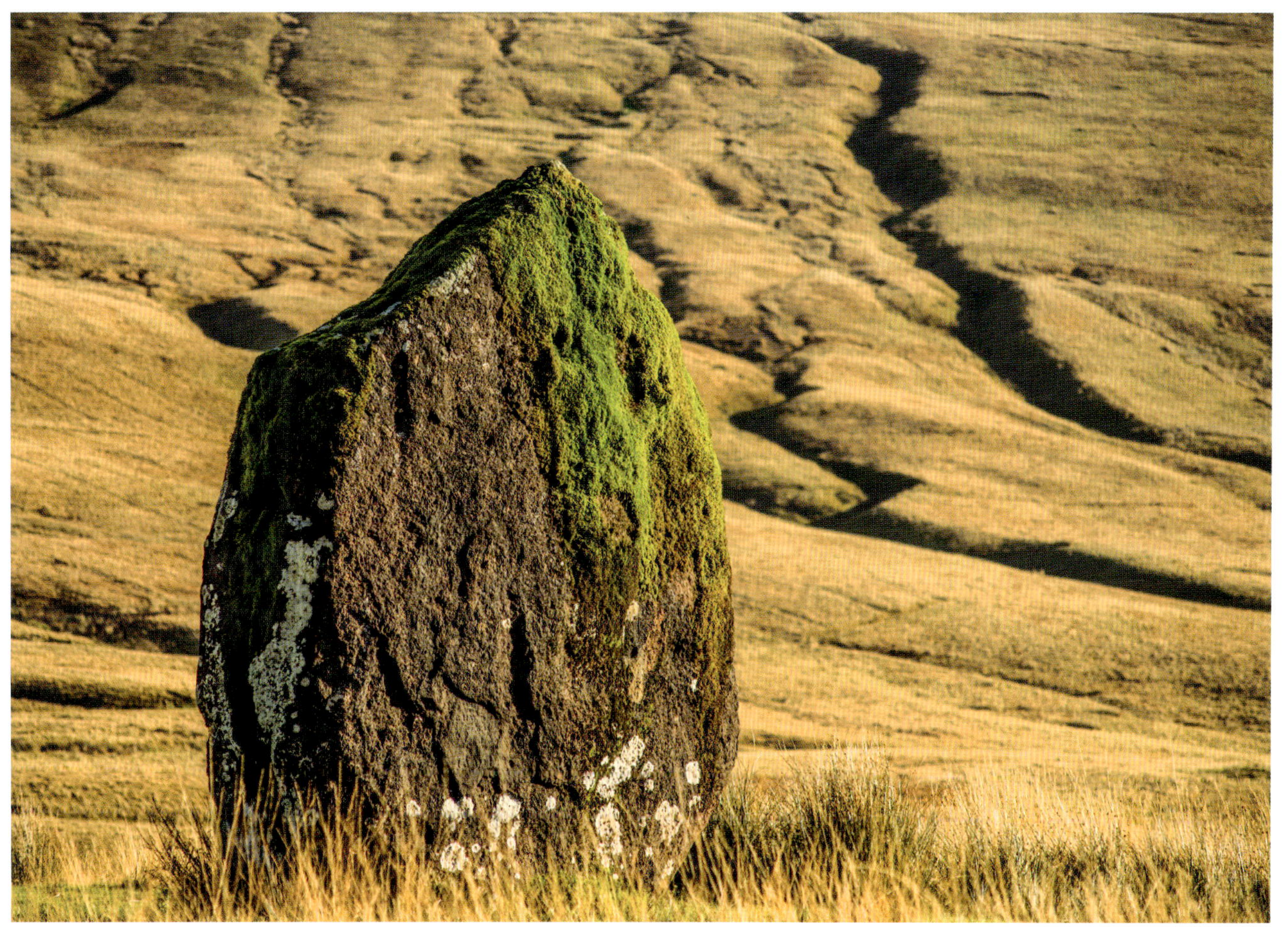

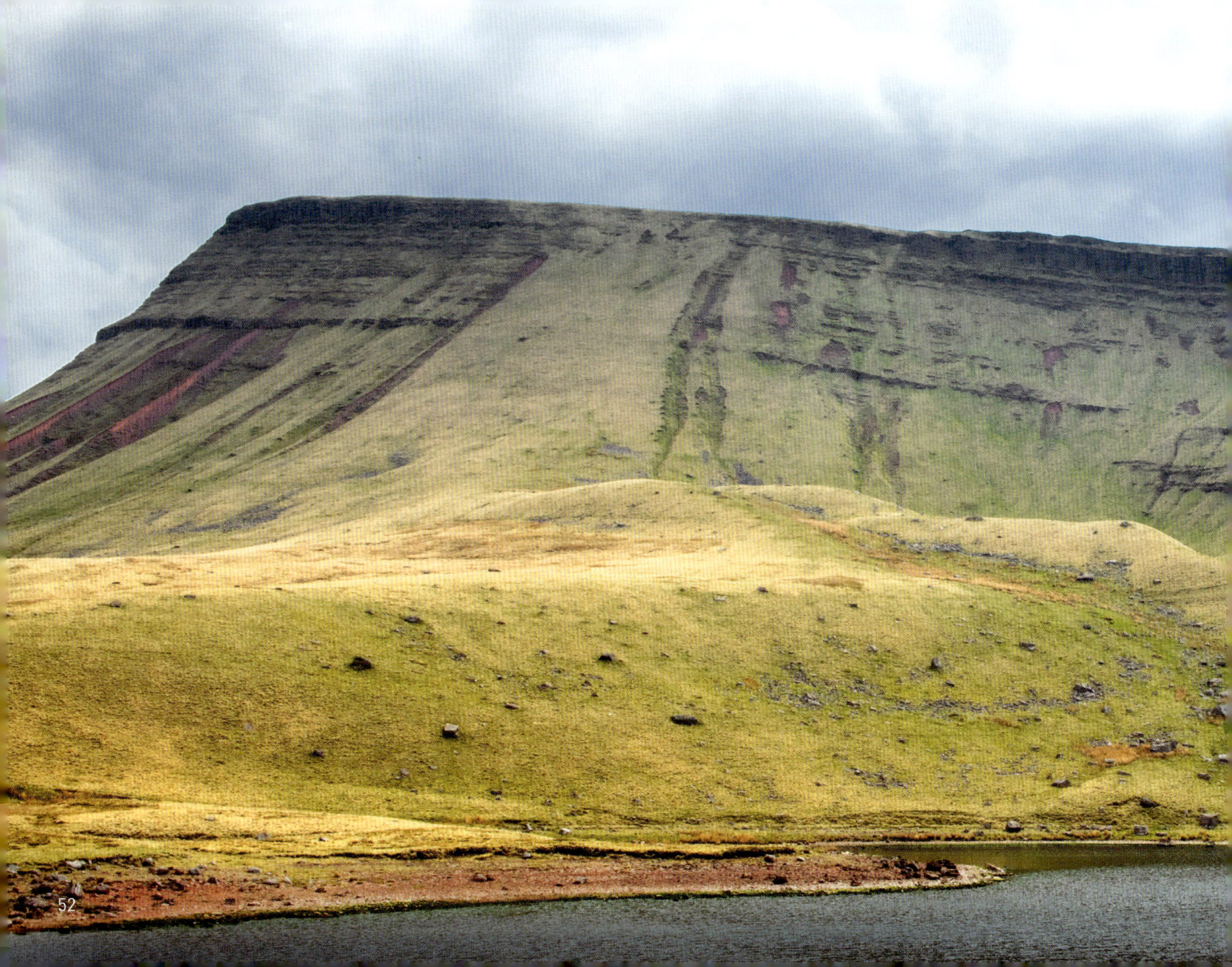

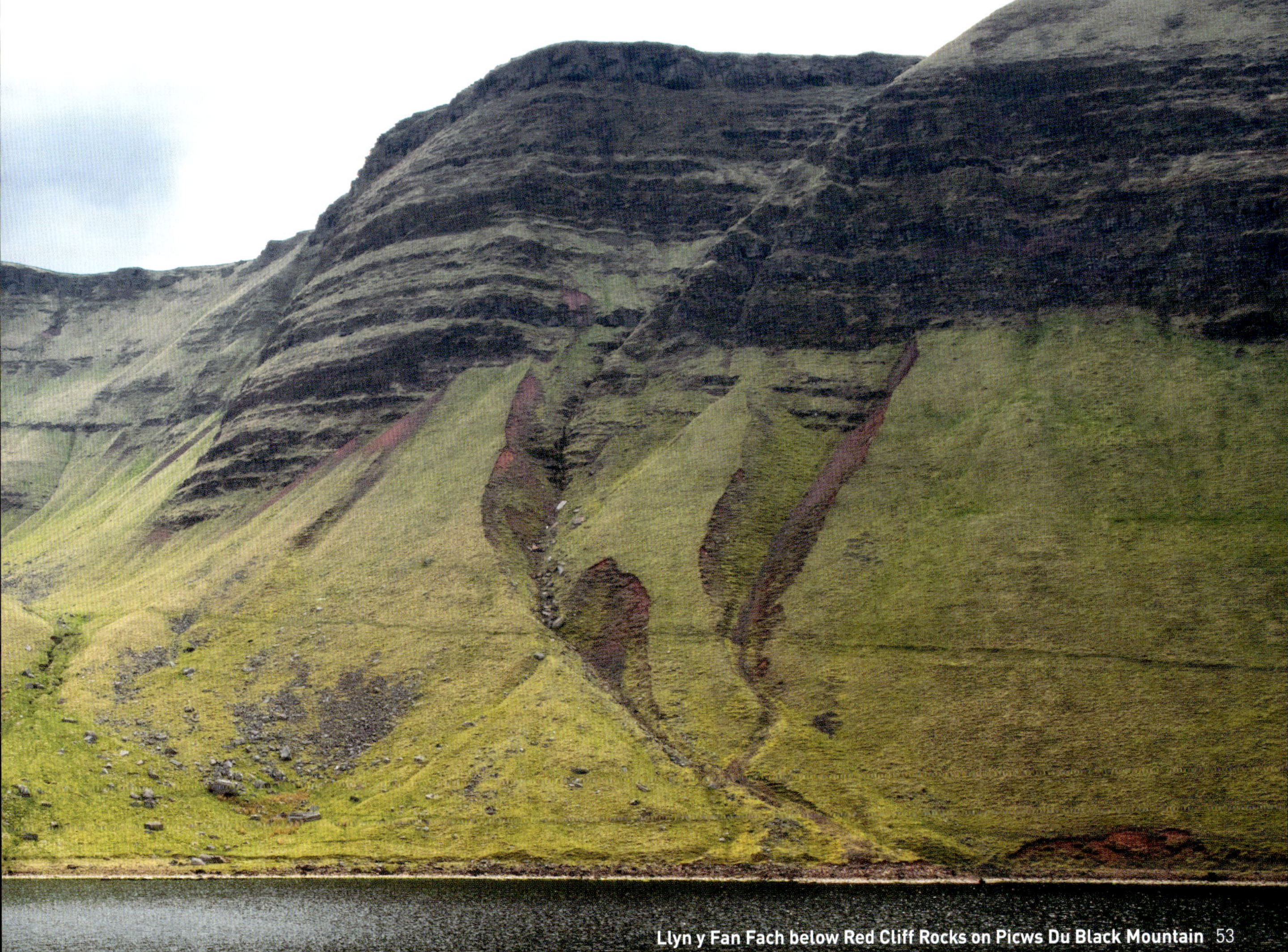

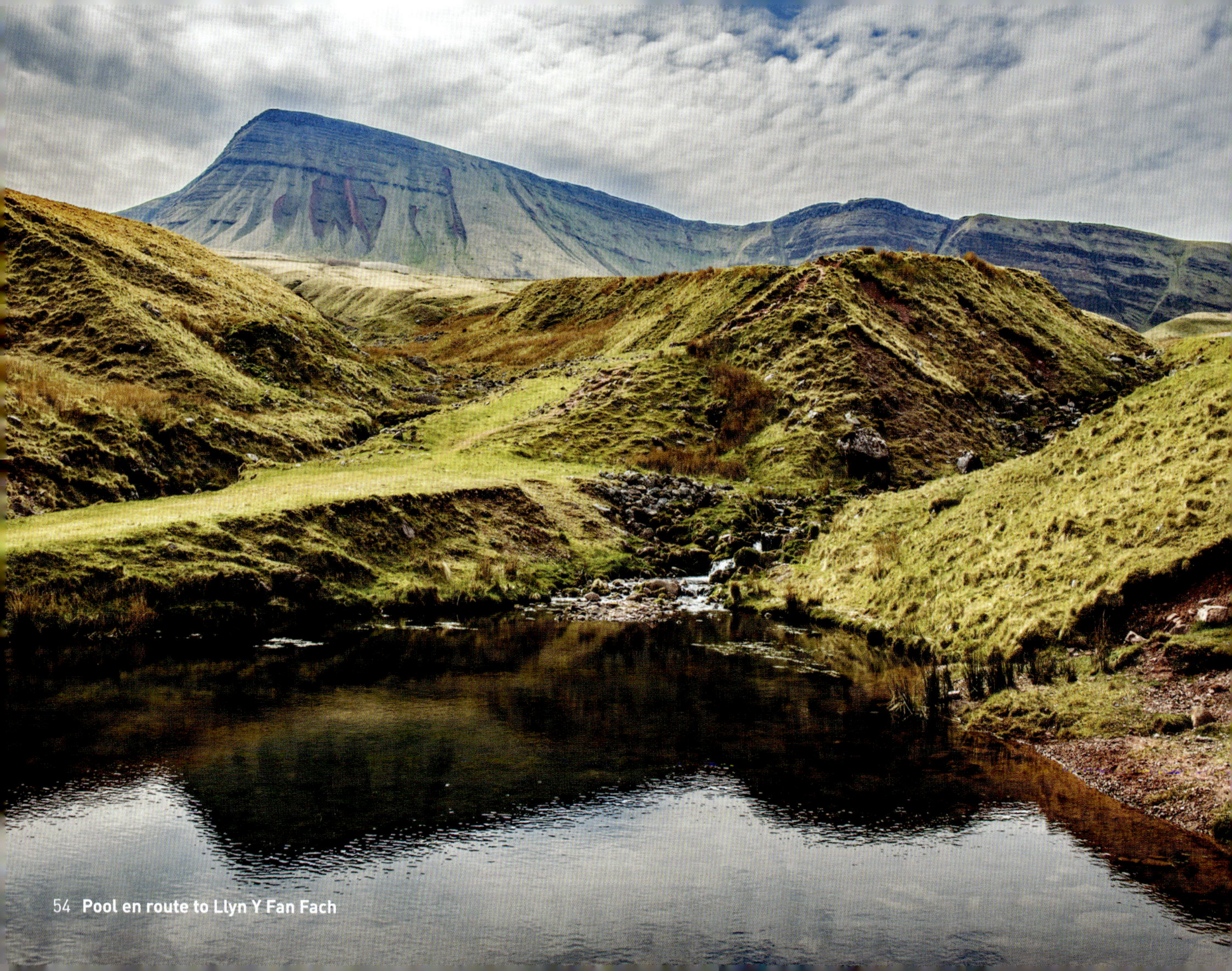

 Pool en route to Llyn Y Fan Fach

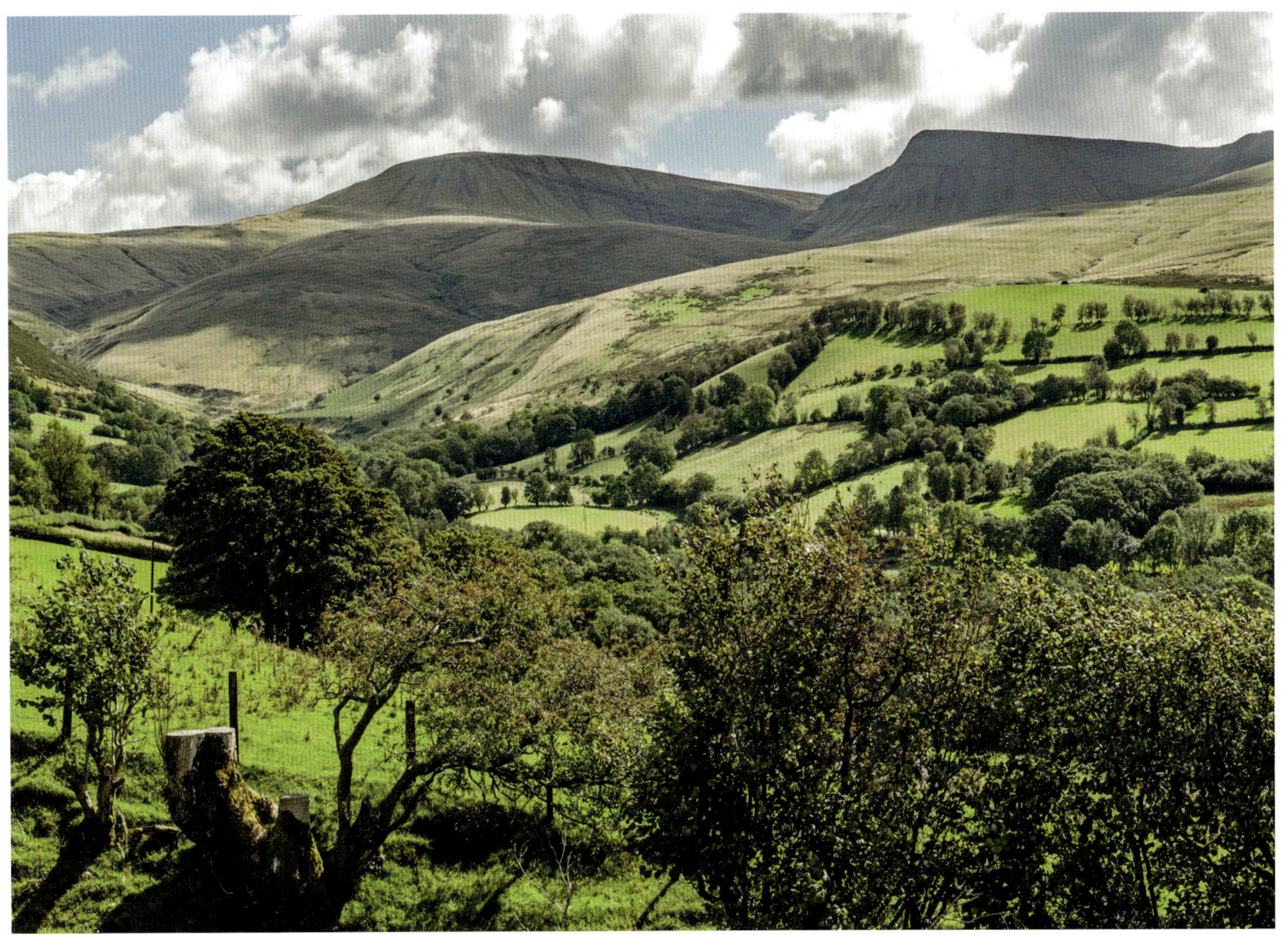

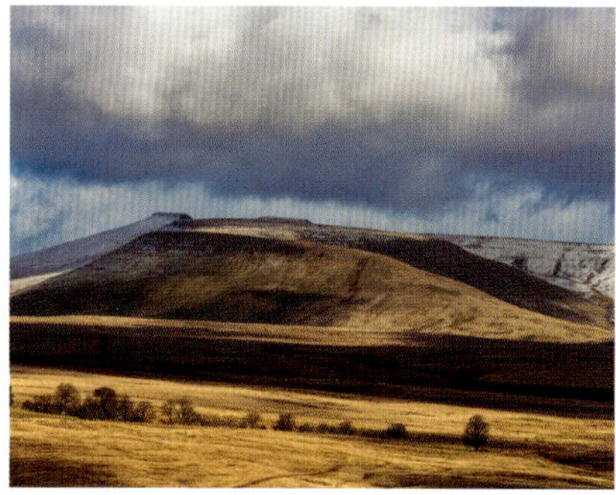

Pages 8-9. This winter view, taken from the A4067, shows Pen y Fan to the left and Corn Du to the right.

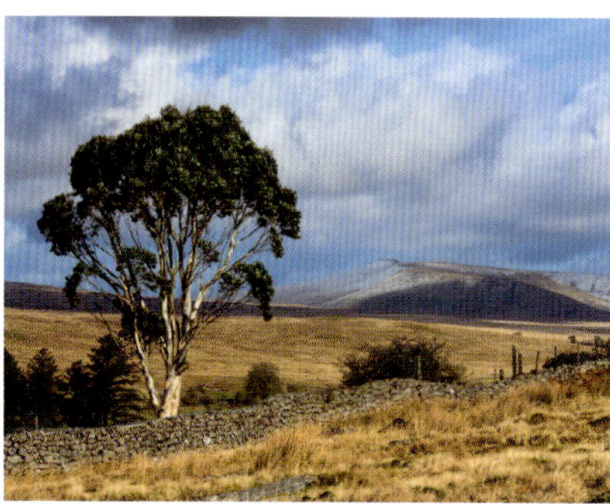

Page 11. To the best of my knowledge this is the only eucalyptus tree in the National Park, standing proudly along the A4067.

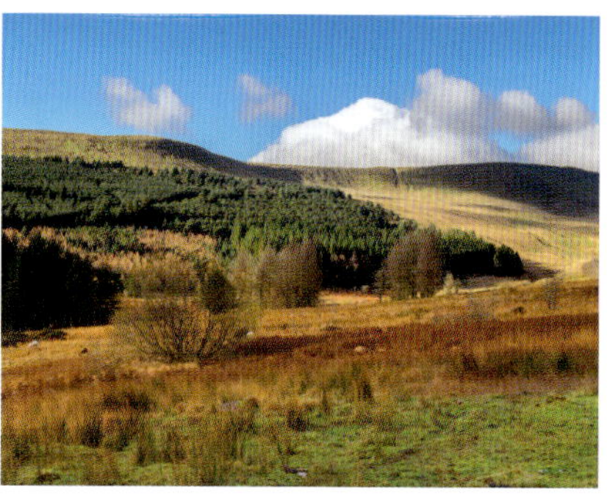

Pages 14-15. A wider perspective from the top of the Taf Fechan Valley shows not only the ridge but also the valley below.

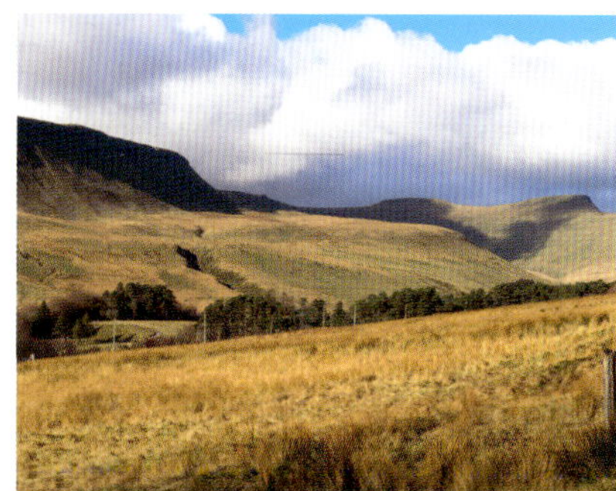

Page 10. The Upper Taf Fechan Valley, with Graig Fan Ddu, Corn Du and Pen y Fan under shadows, sunlight and large, looming clouds.

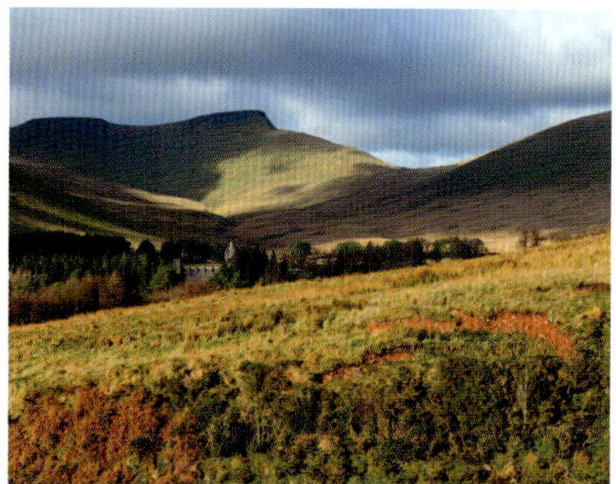

Pages 12-13. Corn Du, Pen y Fan and Cribyn from the very head of the Taf Fechan Valley in the Central Bannau Brycheiniog.

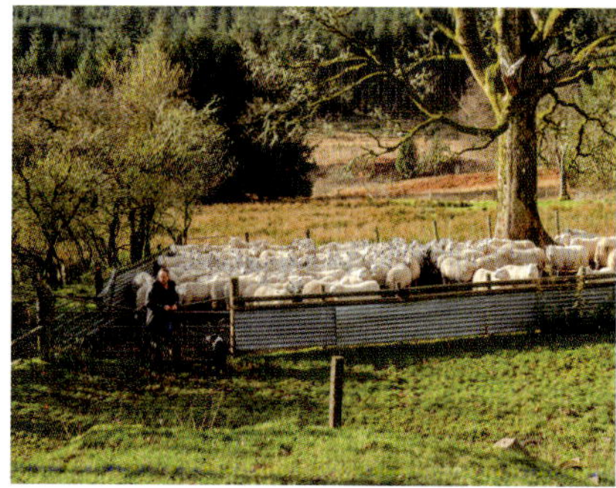

Pages 16-17. A view of a Bannau Brycheiniog sheep farmer who, together with his dog, has successfully penned in his flock.

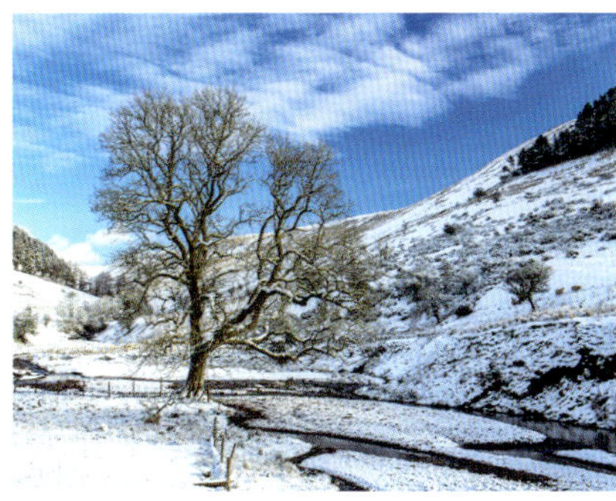

Page 18. An oak tree in the depths of winter, taken at the bottom of the valley of Cwm Crew, just off the A470.

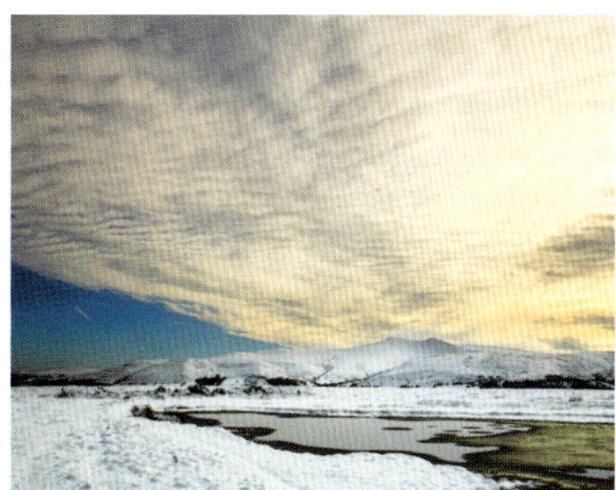

Pages 20-21. This was taken from Mynydd Illtyd Common, which offers beautiful views of the Central Bannau Brycheiniog throughout the whole year.

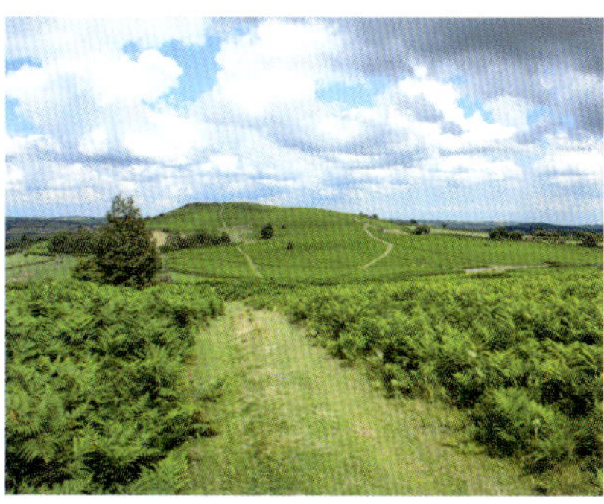

Page 23. Known as the Twyn by locals, the views make it clear why this location was chosen to be a hillfort.

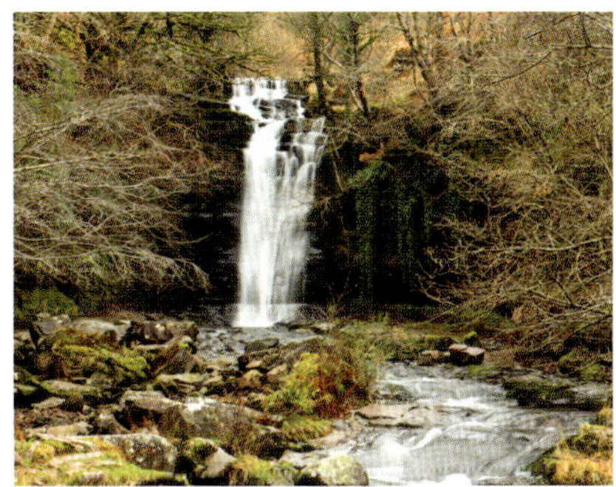

Page 19 The Blaen y Glyn Falls on the River Caerfanell are easy to reach and very popular with outward-bound youngsters.

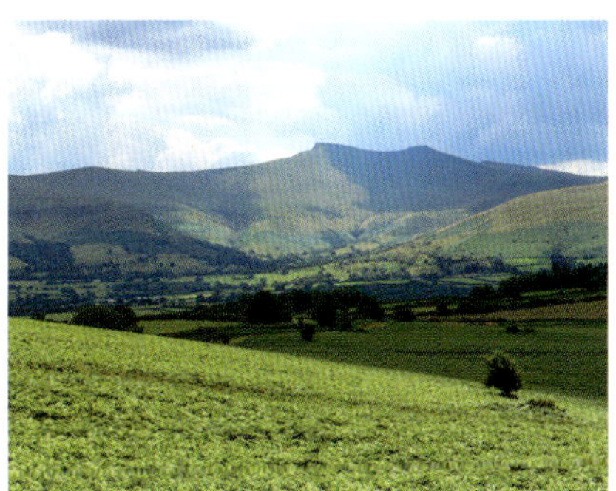

Page 22. This scene from the top of the Twyn y Gaer, an Iron Age hillfort, offers an all-round panorama of much of the Bannau Brycheiniog.

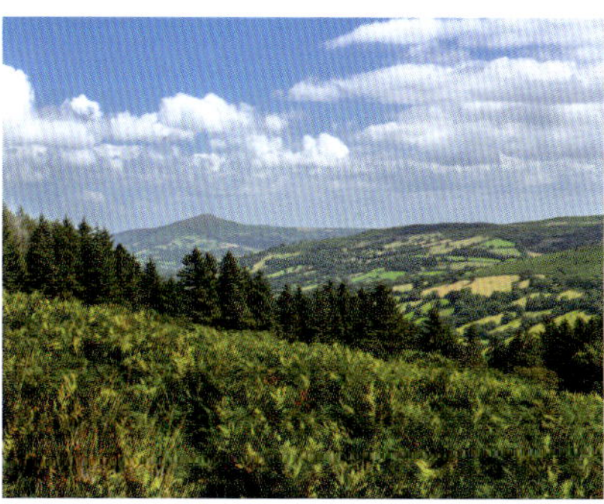

Pages 24-25. At 551m high, Tor y Foel offers a view of Talybont Valley nearby and Sugar Loaf Mountain in east Bannau Brycheiniog.

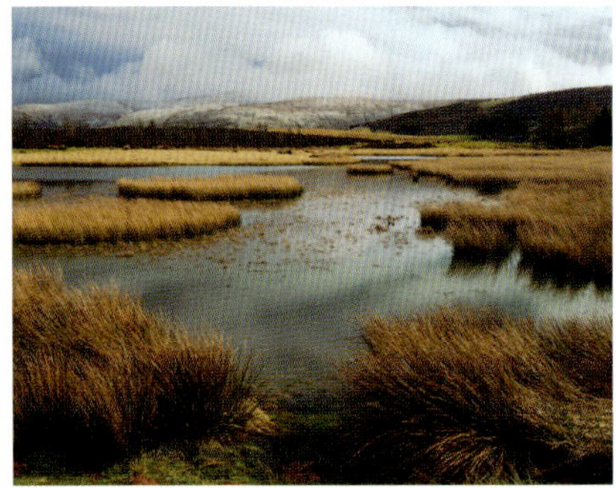

Page 26. The pond high on Mynydd Illtyd Common is well known for harbouring all sorts of insects, though most species are hibernating in this view.

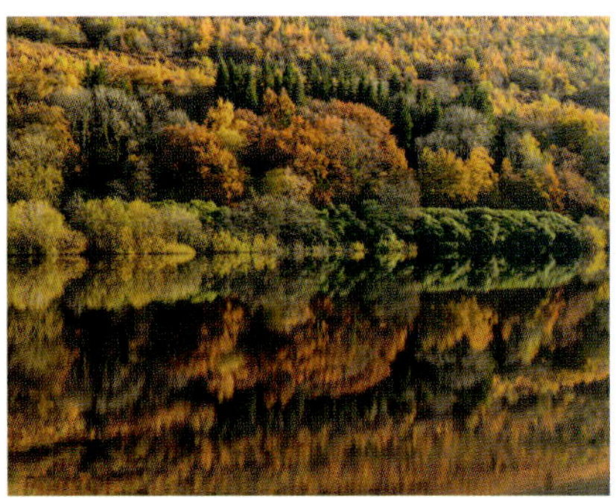

Pages 28-29. Reflections on the beautiful Talybont Reservoir, which takes water from the River Caerfanell and the streams flowing from surrounding hills.

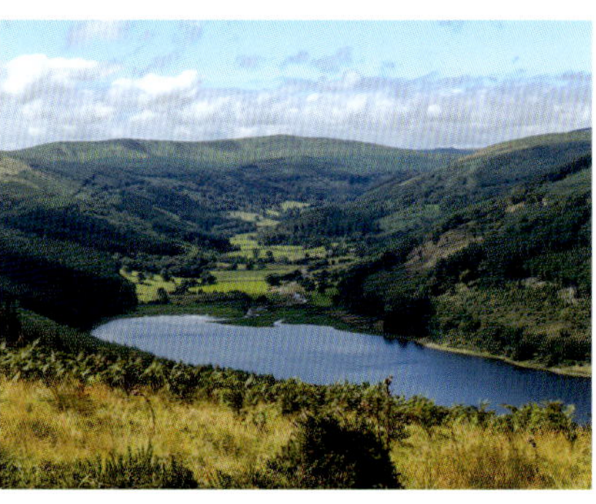

Page 32. A similar photograph taken from Bwlch y Waun, a wonderful spot to simply sit and stare.

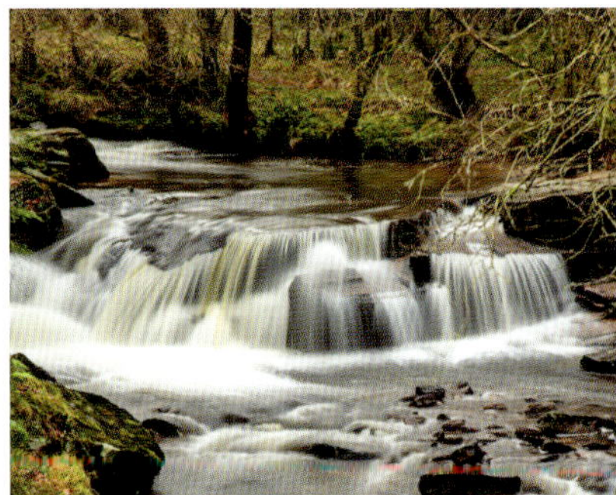

Page 27. Pont Cwm y Fedwen waterfall, with the road making its way up to the top of the Taf Fechan Valley.

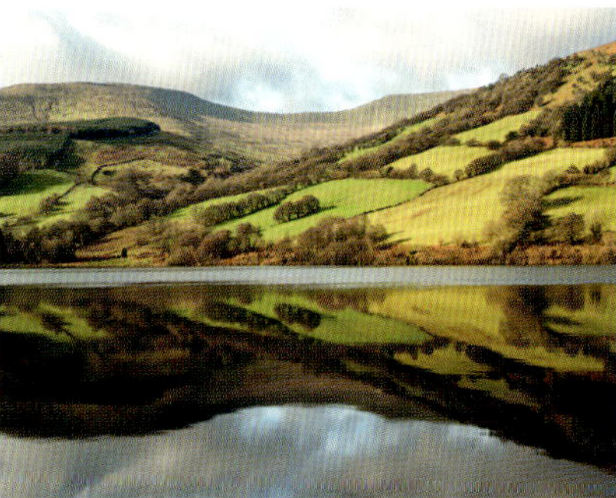

Pages 30-31. I swung round to the west to capture reflections of the hills, trees and fields in Talybont Reservoir.

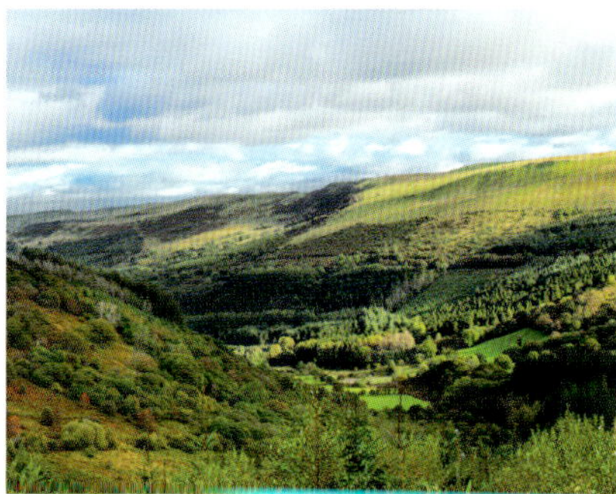

Page 33. The top or upper end of the Talybont Valley, also known as Glyn Collwn, densely covered with both deciduous and evergreen trees.

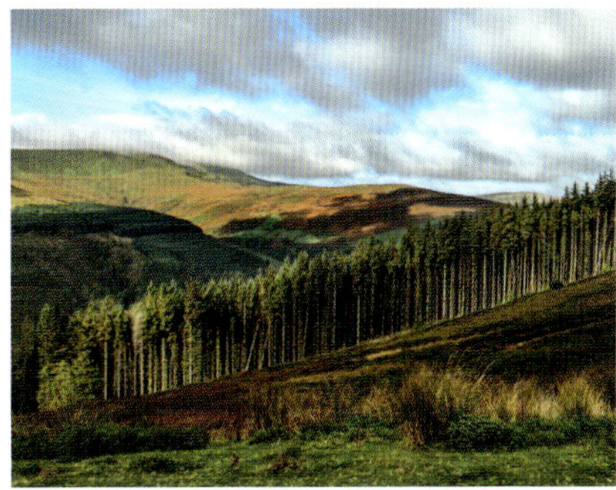

Pages 34-35. One of many amazing views of the Bannau Brycheiniog. This scene looks across the Talybont Reservoir to the mountain of Waun Rydd.

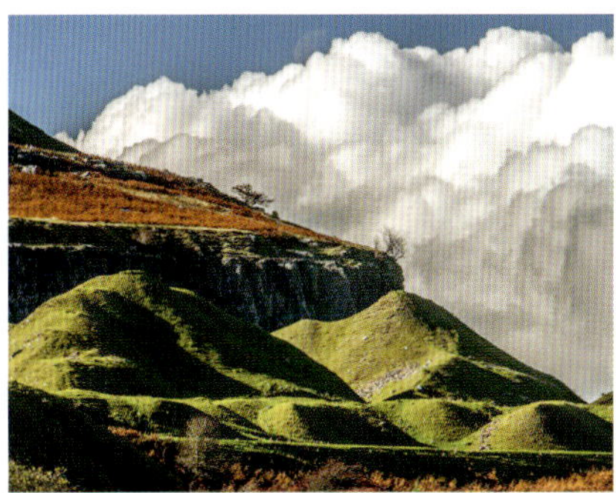

Page 38. This enormous cloud, the largest I've seen, billowed up behind the escarpment as I approached the limestone cliffs and spoil heaps.

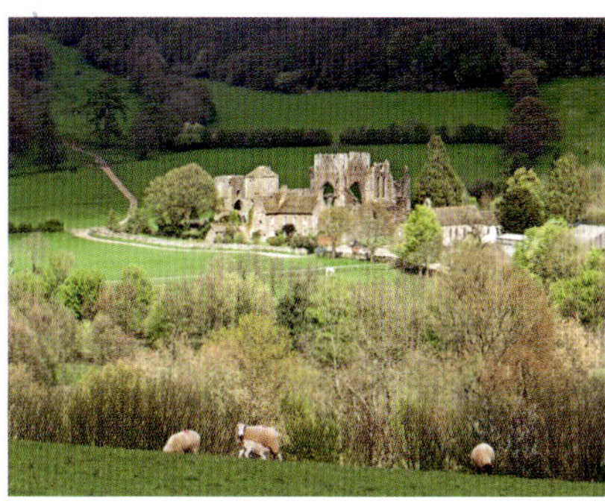

Page 40. Looking down to the ruins of Llanthony Priory, deep in the Vale of Ewyas, from the hillside opposite.

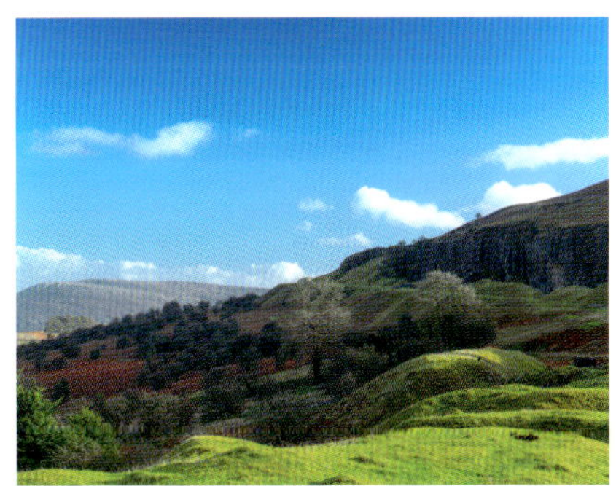

Pages 36-37. Looking along the ridge of Daren Cilau from the Llangattock Escarpment, showing the remains of limestone cliffs.

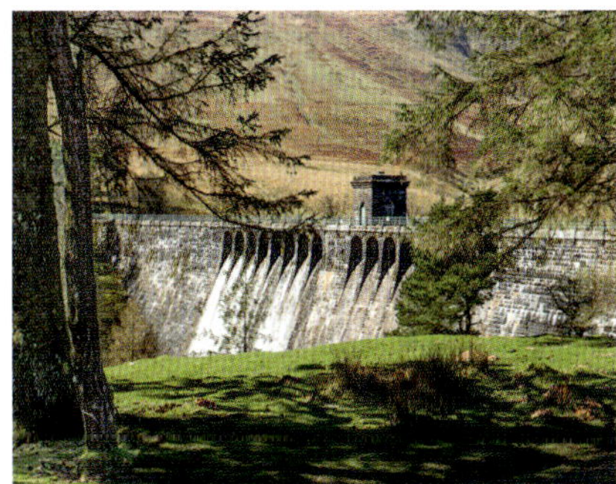

Page 39. The white effect on the reservoir's dam is not water but the result of lime leaching through the stonework near the top.

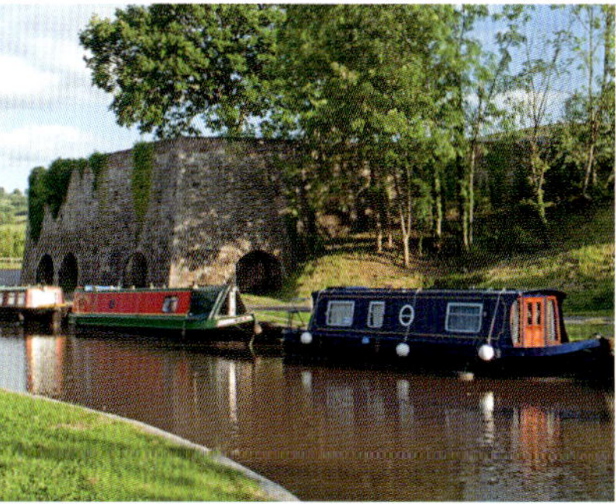

Page 41. Narrowboats moored up on the Brecon and Monmouth Canal. The disused lime kiln was once used to carry lime down to Newport in barges.

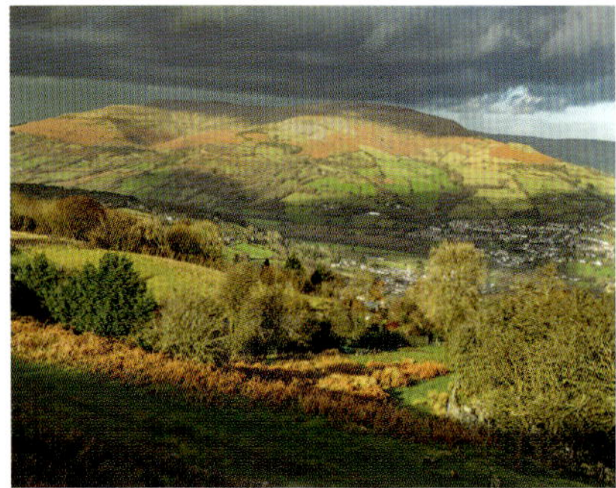

Page 42. Pen Cerrig-calch looms over Crickhowell in the afternoon sunshine. In the distance on its right is Crug Hywel, associated with tenth-century king Hywel Dda.

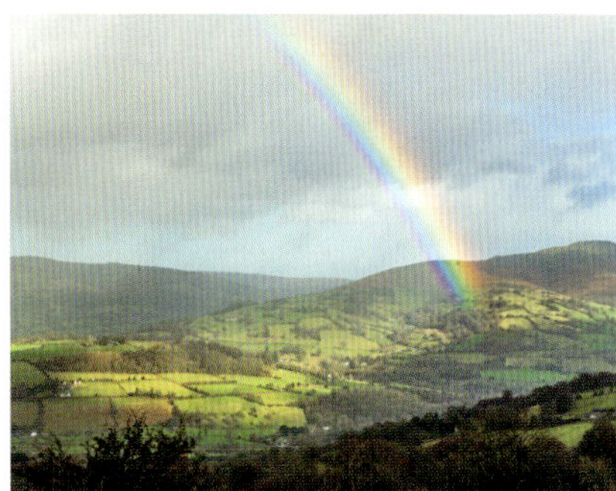

Pages 44-45. A rainbow over the River Usk, one end almost landing on the Sugar Loaf and the rest above the Usk Valley in Monmouthshire.

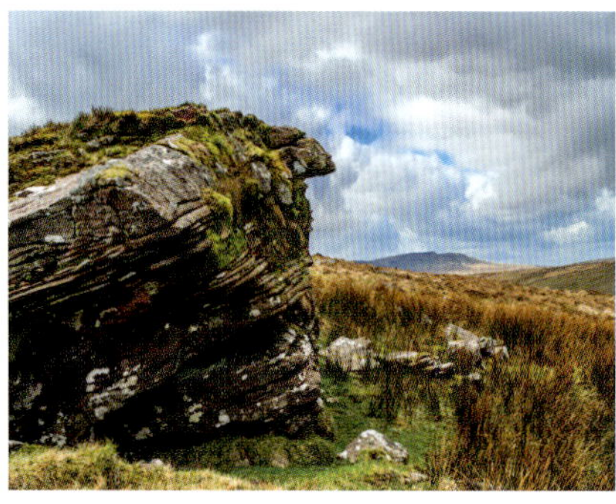

Page 47. From here the view extends west, where you can make out the outline of the Bannau Brycheiniog and the cliffs further on.

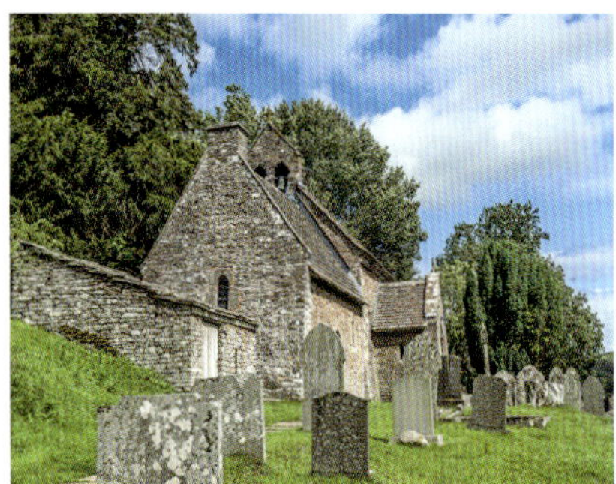

Page 43. The remote St Issui's church, near Partrishow in the Grwyne Fawr Valley, is a Grade 1 listed building and well worth a visit.

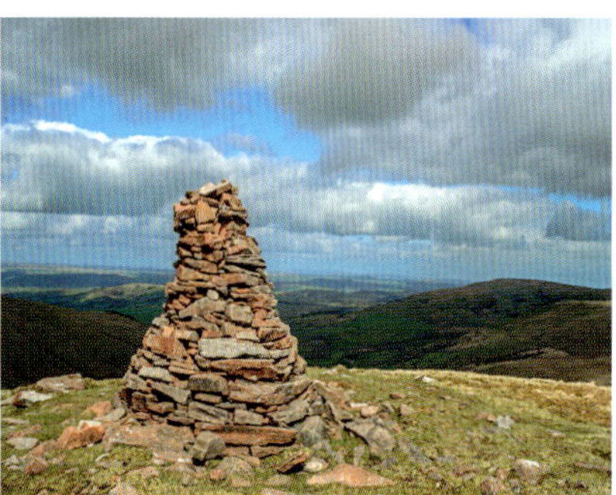

Page 46. Climbing the summit of Fan Nedd on a fair day suddenly opens up amazing views from west Bannau Brycheiniog across to Pen y Fan.

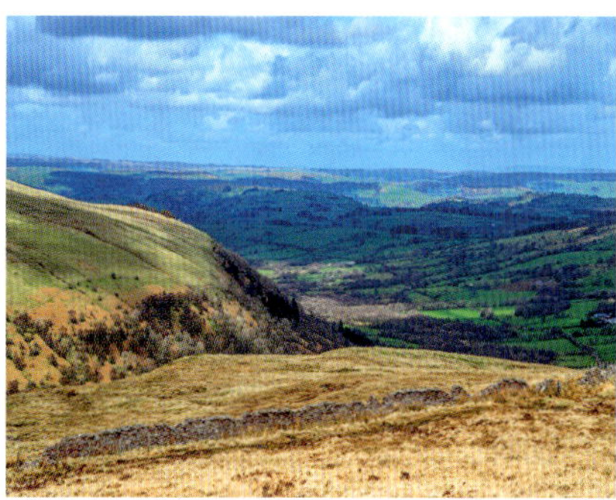

Page 48. The view from the summit of Fan Nedd along the Senni Valley, with its farms and hedgerows, to Heol Senni.

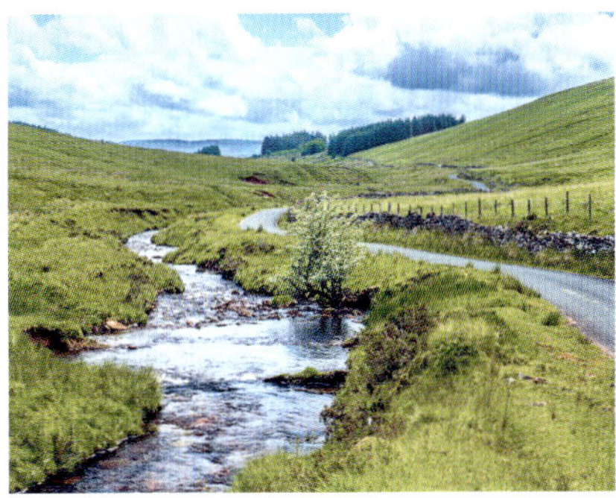

Page 49. This view takes us down the Llia Valley, with forestry in the distance and the winding road making its way south.

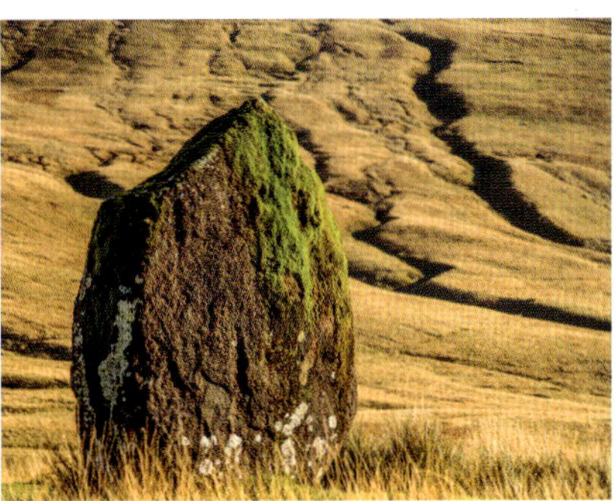

Page 51. Believed to have been erected in the Bronze Age, this upright standing stone in the Llia Valley never fails to draw visitors.

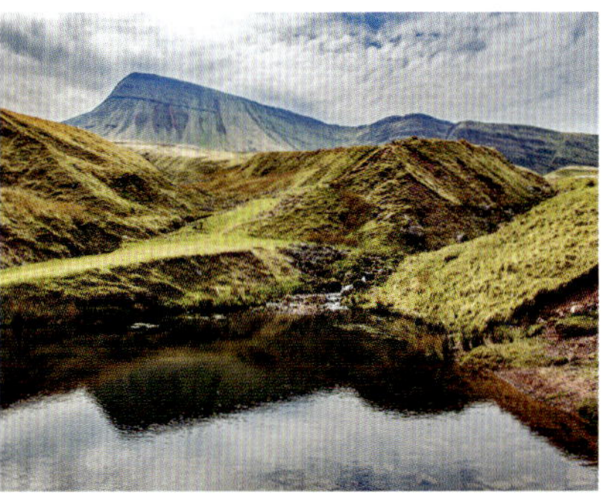

Page 54. Taken on a stormy day from the top of Picws Du, this scene shows the full extent of Llyn y Fan Fach.

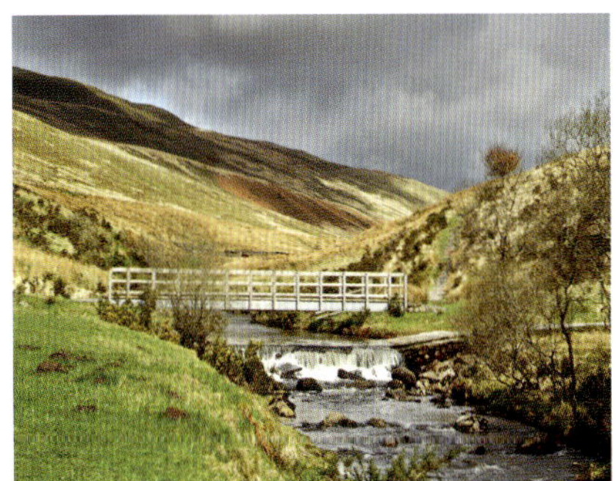

Page 50. The River Llia, responsible for creating the Llia Valley, runs under the bridge and ultimately to the Vale of Neath.

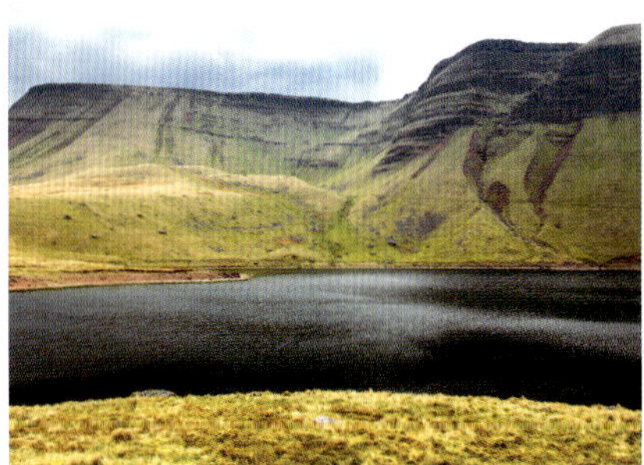

Pages 52-53. A westerly view of the high ridge over Llyn y Fan Fach, again showing the colour and nature of the rock hereabouts.

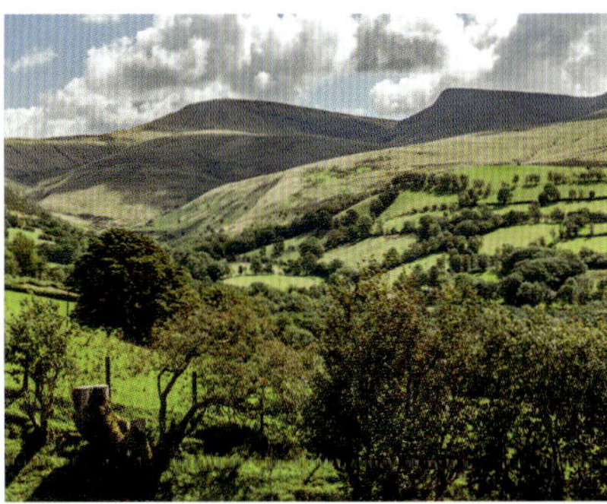

Page 55. To the left is Ban Brycheiniog, with Picws Du next along. Below the summit of Picws Du lies Llyn y Fan Fach.

Nick Jenkins

For a number of years now I have pursued landscape photography all over the UK and abroad. My passion for landscapes grew, I guess, from my love of the countryside in general. When I was young, I was the proud owner of a small and inexpensive camera which went almost everywhere with me. This became a bit of an attachment after a while, and once I became a teenager I had a better camera for my birthday from my father. It was a Zenit E film camera, and to its credit it gave me some very good photographs from the film. The lenses were all screw in though, not bayonet fits like we have today.

My next leap took place when I was asked by my employers if I would take the photographs for the next year's calendar. Phew, they had such faith in me! Luckily, all went well, and they even paid me for my trouble!

I have walked and photographed in a number of UK National Parks, including the Bannau Brycheiniog, Eryri, the Pembrokeshire Coast, the Lake District and the Yorkshire Dales and Moors as well as open rural countryside around parts of the UK coastline, including the Cornish coast and the Isles of Scilly. I have also been extremely fortunate to have both visited and run photography workshops in these UK locations as well as pursuing my own opportunities in parts of Italy, India, Nepal, Slovakia, Croatia, Iceland, Switzerland, France, Czech Republic, the Isles of Scilly, and a number of others.

I was also commissioned to photograph the Isle of Man for the Manx Tourism Department.

Whilst I love all and any forms of outdoor photography, I should confess here that I also have two specific aims in my mind.

These are:

1. To visit, explore and photograph as many National Parks as I am able, as many Country Parks as I can and to capture the wildness and beauty of the coast of the UK, some of which falls under National Park jurisdiction, and

2. To help fellow photographers, professional or budding, to use their cameras and lenses to best effect, to seek out and isolate locations of beauty with elements that will hold the viewer's eye and

stir up interest. I do this on a 1:1 basis over a day or with a group over a week.

All that said, I also have a real love for the country so I seek out and explore woodlands, forests, rivers, waterfalls, legally accessible countryside, and any other beautiful outdoor locations I can find. Nowhere is safe from me.

I must confess, the Bannau Brycheiniog National Park has so much to offer in terms of rugged landscapes, high hills, waterfalls and deep valleys that I could reasonably spend ages and ages here and still, in all probability, miss something!

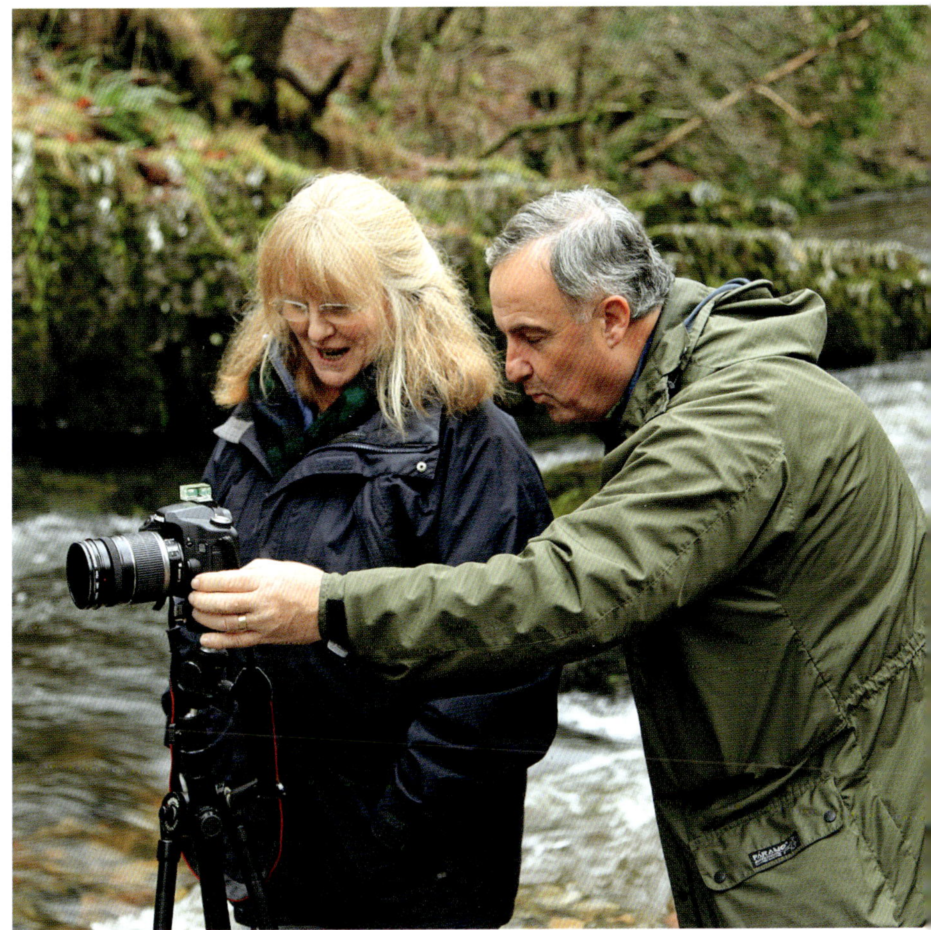

National Parks of Wales Series

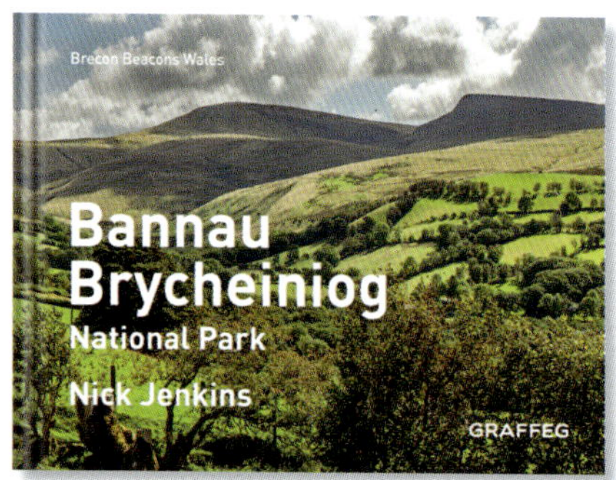

ISBN 9781802582031

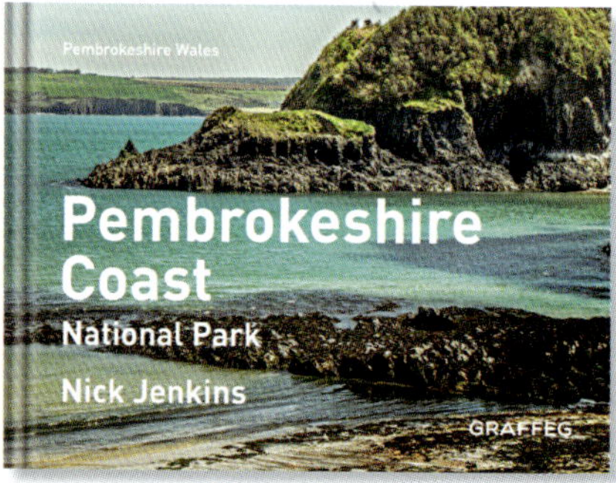

ISBN 9781802587258

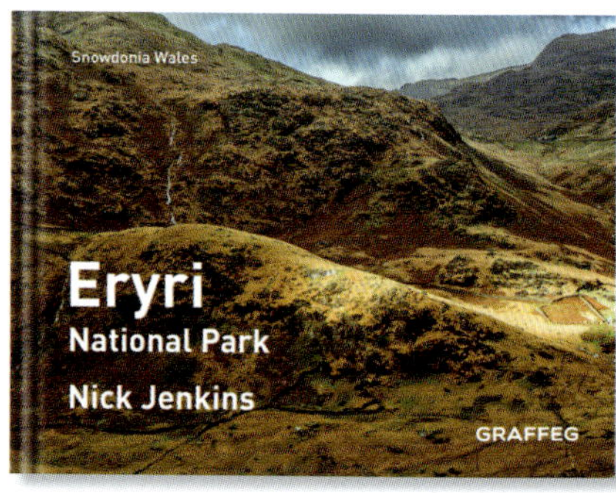

ISBN 9781802587241

In the National Parks of Wales series, photographer Nick Jenkins shares his favourite images and locations from Bannau Brycheiniog, Eryri and Pembrokeshire Coast National Parks.

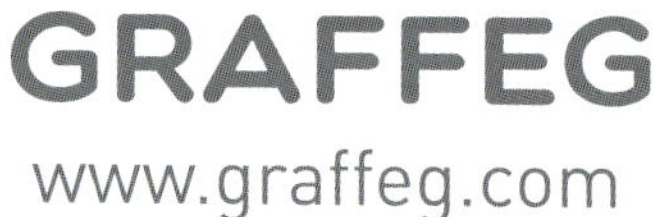

www.graffeg.com

National Parks of Wales
Series